PRAISE FOR *CAMP GRANDMA*

"Over the river and through the woods to a totally different kind of grandmother! In this unique and wonderful book, Day offers a new and refreshing perspective on being a twenty-first-century grandmother. Readers will experience an enjoyable story *and* gain ideas and creative ways of helping their own grandchildren grow strong, think critically, and have fun all at the same time. Funny, wise, clever, practical, and helpful, *Camp Grandma* presents a new layer to consider in the relationship between grand-parent and grandchild."

—LAREE KIELY, PhD, President, WeWill, Inc.

"By sharing her life experiences, Marianne Waggoner Day demonstrates how to engage our grandchildren in meaningful opportunities to build their personal skills, as well as their loving relationships with each other and their families, while having fun at the same time. She opens our eyes to what it means to bring our whole life's experiences to the art of being a grandparent and offers insightful and real-life examples of how to make a positive contribution as a 'grandma' in the lives of four very different grandchildren. She shows us that the time today's active and capable grandparents spend with their grandchildren can be an enriching and impactful experience that goes well beyond our traditional view of grandparents as 'babysitters.'"

—NANCY J. LAVELLE, PhD, founder and President/CEO, Total Education Solutions, Inc.

"In a time when mobility, social media, and rootlessness characterize the experience of so many of our children, Marianne Waggoner Day describes a wonderful approach that draws on the wisdom of a former era."

—JOYCE CROFOOT, PhD, clinical psychologist

"An entertaining and effective way to build constructive, long-term relationships with your grandchildren. Good for grandmothers—and grandfathers, too."

—ROBERT LEECH, financial planner and grandfather

"*Camp Grandma* not only is a terrific story of how to make the most of your relationships with your grandchildren but also sheds light on the role of grandparents and how we are valued in our society. With a smart and unique perspective on grandparenting, Day uses her experience to connect with her grandchildren and establishes Camp Grandma, a program she created for her grandchildren to teach them about the world we live in. In her book, Day takes the reader on this heartwarming, intelligent, and funny journey to her awareness of the importance of grandparenting and the passing on of information, knowledge, and wisdom to the new generation."

—JULIE ANNE PERKINS, former educator and mindfulness instructor

"*Camp Grandma* has a positive and uplifting energy that encourages and inspires this longtime teacher and brand-new grandma to open her heart to new adventures, new learning, and new loves with her grandchild."

—SUSAN SNYDER, MS Ed, education specialist; general education and special education teacher; Adjunct Instructor, University of La Verne; and new grandma

"Delightfully written with clarity and humor, *Camp Grandma* is a wise and inspirational book for grandparents and grandparents-to-be. It's packed with great ideas you can customize for grandchildren of any age. It's a resource I'll turn to again and again."

—JO BONITA RAINS, educator and cultural diversity specialist

"This book gives grandparents an insightful look and guide to help their grandchildren's development and find value and purpose in their lives while giving them a new sense of value and purpose in their own—an essential need for healthy human existence for all generations. A truly remarkable book that redefines what it means to be a grandparent and gives grandchildren the skills they need to last a lifetime."

—LUCINDA A. RIBANT, MFT, marriage and family therapist

"As Marianne Waggoner Day eloquently describes her precious camp, one realizes that a grandparent can shed the rules and restrictions that accompany parenthood. Additionally, her camp is seen through the lens of a corporate person—one who encourages playing and working together and problem solving toward common goals."

—MICHELE A. WAGMAN, speech and language pathologist

CAMP GRANDMA

CAMP GRANDMA

Next-Generation Grandparenting—
BEYOND BABYSITTING

MARIANNE WAGGONER DAY

SHE WRITES PRESS

Published 2019
Printed in the United States of America
ISBN: 978-1-63152-511-7
ISBN: 978-1-63152-512-4
Library of Congress Control Number: 2018958906

For information, address:
She Writes Press
1569 Solano Ave #546
Berkeley, CA 94707

She Writes Press is a division of SparkPoint Studio, LLC.

Cover and interior design by Tabitha Lahr

For my family, with all my love

All, everything that I understand, I understand only because I love.

—*Leo Tolstoy,* War and Peace

CONTENTS

PREFACE

I originally considered calling this book "Please Don't Call Me a Babysitter." Not because I have anything against babysitters—heck, I regularly care for my grandchildren in the absence of their parents. I resist the term because it doesn't begin to describe what grandparents are to our grandchildren. I contend we do far more than just "babysit," though that has become a term I often hear nowadays in the context of time grandparents spend with their grandchildren. Consider instead that along with being caretakers, we are role models, teachers, historians, storytellers, confidants, mentors, and most importantly, trusted examples of how to love and be loved.

Of course, I didn't understand the potential of the role when my first grandchild was born. I was at the top of my thirty-plus-year career as a business executive. I continued working five more years (and welcoming several more grandchildren) before I elected to step down from my management position—I wanted to take my foot off the corporate gas pedal, so to speak (still unaware of what was in store for me as a grandparent).

For retirement, my intention was to focus more on myself, a common choice for women who have worked for years trying to have it all, family and career. I started planning for my retirement years. The theme would be balance. I would enjoy the freedom to take better care of my health, exercise on a regular basis, start meditating, and reconnect with my friends and social relations, while staying professionally active with some consulting and business coaching assignments. Oh yes, and travel! It all sounds great, right? A nice balance to it. I felt quite confident that my last chapter was well-defined and sensibly planned out.

But my plans changed. I found something more compelling and much more rewarding: my grandkids.

I knew I wouldn't be content with being just a babysitter to my grandchildren: playing simple games with them, watching them play in the park for hours, sitting with them as they colored at my kitchen table. Since I was a businesswoman with a tendency to go all in, I went all in with my grandchildren, mining what I learned in the corporate world for their benefit. The result was Camp Grandma, where I teach my grandchildren about the world we live in, as you will see from the activities outlined in this book.

But my grandchildren have taught me as well, perhaps more, if truth be told. I have learned some unexpected and invaluable lessons from them. This reciprocal learning between us—this exchange of wisdoms and experiences—has enriched my life, along with the lives of my grandchildren, measurably and immeasurably.

I didn't recognize the symbiotic relationship between kids and grandparents before I had grandchildren. And it didn't hit me all at once. It took time being in their good company. They opened my eyes. When they were born, I knew I would love them. After all, they're the children of my own two children. But did I understand the power of this perfect match? No way—I didn't see it coming.

Maybe it's because of this special symmetry I've discovered between grandparents and grandchildren, and the fact of it being such a revelation, that I have to share it. When such riches lie just under the surface—almost in plain sight—we must be encouraged to see them. There is potential to be fulfilled in our later years, more than I ever imagined. And if you're a grandparent, it's right there under your nose.

INTRODUCTION:

A PERFECT MATCH

Kids are so smart. In fact, the only people smarter are old people. So right away with us, they've met their match. Kids start life without any filters or rules. They see—or feel—what's true and act on impulse without worrying what other people will think. Old people (and I still cringe at that description of myself, but hey, it is what it is) embrace life much the same way. We have cast off the filters and useless rules accumulated throughout adulthood that kept us from moving more freely in the world. So we've got some things in common with kids: a high degree of perceptivity and a love of freedom. We've got one up on them though in that we know what's coming next for them, which is why we're in a perfect position to mentor, coach, and prepare kids for what lies ahead.

And with kids, let's face it, we've met our match. They see right through us, so where kids are concerned, we have to keep it honest. Any pretense or canned behavior is out. You'll lose them fast if all you're doing is an act. Don't rob them of the real you by playing to the crowd. Be with them. Be real. They can spot a phony a mile away, which is an extra benefit since we can be ourselves completely, warts and all. That's quite freeing in itself for kids to see. They can realize that, wow, a person can be his or her unique self. They can be flawed and make mistakes and still be accepted, functioning, even cool and lovable. Kids want you to love them and pay attention to them. So, if you're there and listening to them and looking at them, at least some of the time, you'll have a friend for life.

What a gift it is to find this perfect match in old age. What an opportunity! How can we make the most of it? It's time we focus on the grandparenting role today, its possibilities, how it should be valued, and the way the women's movement of the last sixty years has reinvigorated and reshaped not only women's approach to being a grandmother but men's approach to the grandfather role, as well. Women now have a broader platform of experiences to share and men are more involved with childcare than ever before. So when I hear other grandparents say, "I'm babysitting my grandchildren," I smile and think to myself, "You are likely doing so much more than babysit!" Babysitters do necessary and important work, caring for kids while their parents are at work or temporarily away. But the grandparent-grandchild relationship is so incredibly special, limitless, and compelling that it changes the childcare dynamic from the stereotypical babysitting job to a much richer and more meaningful experience.

So, of course grandparents do some babysitting, but next time you are caring for your grandchildren in the absence of their parents, take a pause. Be mindful of your influence and unique relationship. Consider sharing more of yourself—your wisdom and your experiences. Go beyond babysitting and be interactive, fully engaged and connected—why set limits on the positive role you can play in the family? Be a mentor to your grandchildren. In contrast to babysitting, mentoring is a commitment of the full and loving self. So who better than the grandparent to help grandchildren grow and develop, significantly improving their chances for a good life?

This book is about how my retirement turned out differently than I expected, how I came to embrace my role as grandmother, using my work-life experiences to connect with my grandchildren and enrich our relationships along the way, as well as how Camp Grandma creatively and organically came to life.

Part 1 of the book reveals a bit about my personal history and the genesis of Camp Grandma. I also discuss how grandparenting is perceived today, as well as my relationship with my own grandparents.

Part 2 gets down to the nuts and bolts of Camp Grandma, which I liken to a corporate retreat for kids. Each chapter contains instructions for educational activities you can do with your grandchildren that cover subjects from goal setting to teamwork. I even discuss the importance of maintaining a good reputation in a world increasingly interconnected by social media and other technology. You can replicate each activity as is or customize it for your grandkids based on their ages and interests. You'll see how you can build upon your own experience, whatever it is, and offer something special to a grandchild. And if you don't have the luxury of living close by, take heart. This book will help you find your way to that connection, whether it's over the phone via Skype, during a weekend visit, or within a few hours of an afternoon.

Part 3 tells about a few of the lessons I've learned from being a grandmother—especially what I've learned from my grandkids about trust and being open to new experiences. I also acknowledge how I've changed as a result.

My story reveals how babysitting can be turned into mentoring. But this is not a how-to on being a good grandparent. Grandparents have already raised their families and know how it is done. This is a celebration of the role and what it means to bring our whole lives' experiences to the art of being a grandparent. It's about opportunity—our opportunity to make a difference in the world by connecting with the young. Most of us, especially as we get older, would like to continue to feel we're making a contribution to the world through community and family. Where better to invest your time than with the newest generation? Your contribution to them will last through their lifetimes. Your investment of energy will pay off for the longest foreseeable extent of time.

There is no one right way to grandparent. All grandparents bring their own unique background and skills into play when they spend time with their grandchildren.

Coming from a business background, I used my life lessons, and you will bring yours to discover your own path to more meaningful and enriching relationships with your grandchildren.

PART 1.
THE INSPIRATION

In the beginning

CHAPTER ONE:

THE GENESIS OF CAMP GRANDMA

I admit it: I started out as a babysitter with my grand-children. When they were infants I was an extra pair of arms to hold, change, feed, or burp them. I'd help the newborns get to sleep so Mom and Dad could get a couple of hours' rest for themselves. I knew how demanding those early weeks are on a young family, so I was more than happy to lend a hand.

I had never given much thought to becoming a grand-parent. I guess I assumed it would happen one day, just as I assumed as a young girl that I would eventually get married and have children of my own. It's a rather traditional and typical unfolding of events, it's true, so I was thrilled when my daughter and her husband had a son—my first grand-child, Jack, who I proudly announced would be the future leader of world peace! At that time, I was still working and was deeply involved with my career. As president of retail services for CBRE, I led the largest commercial retail real estate practice in the world. Under my management, our company outperformed the competition nearly two to one. Over my career this translated to having globally managed, leased, sold, valued, financed, or advised assets in excess of $190 billion. I was the first woman to earn the company's prestigious Lifetime Achievement award at the one-hundred-year-old firm. So it was fun to see Jack when I could, and I was happy to help with his care on occasion, but I was still in the throes of my own busy life.

My situation was much the same, workwise, when Jake—the first child of my son and his wife—came along two years later. Once again, I was lucky to be there and share in the joy and miracle of his birth.

A year later came Katie—Jack's sister. Two years later came Lauren—Jake's sister. Five years later came Kate, and just recently Paige arrived. They are the daughters of my stepson and his wife. At this time, I have six grandchildren, counting my husband's (and I do!). I regularly care for and spend time with the four oldest, and they are the characters who came to populate Camp Grandma. (The two youngest are from my second marriage and live some distance away, but they have two wonderful other grandmothers who live nearby.)

I started taking care of my four grandchildren on a regular basis during the summer, about five years into my retirement, when Jack was ten, Jake eight, Katie seven, and Lauren five. Taking the name from a picture frame I saw at

Target, we began to call our time together Camp Grandma. When it first started that summer, I had T-shirts made for us all with "Camp Grandma" written across the fronts, but I had no idea what would happen next.

I handed each of them a shirt on the first day of Camp Grandma, asking them all to put them on.

They held the shirts up, one by one, to get a better look. Jake immediately put his down, shook his head, and politely said, "Uh, uh . . . no, thank you."

"What's this?" the littler girls asked.

"Oh, pretty, mine's like yours, Katie," said Lauren.

"Why do I have to wear this? I already have a shirt on!" exclaimed Jack.

I defended my purchase. "Well, I thought it would be fun to wear matching T-shirts since we're all sharing this experience together. See, I've got one on too."

Jack, still skeptical, put his on. The girls jumped up and down exclaiming, "We're twins!" and Jake set his shirt down again and took off to find something else to do.

Now what? I ran down the stairs to the garage to see what in the world I could find that might be of interest to them. The first thing I spotted was a flip chart on its stand and I grabbed it. A holdover from my corporate days, the familiarity of it gave me an idea. It all starts with a plan, right?

I lugged the thing up the stairs and called the kids to the kitchen table. They gathered round, and I provided them with a basic outline of an agenda. (Note that if you're following along and want to set your own grandkids up with an agenda, you don't have to have a flip chart. You can use regular paper, construction paper, a white board, or anything else you have around the house.)

"How do you want to spend your time today?" I asked. "What do we want to accomplish from our time together?" I was standing in front of the flip chart like I had in my career, leading a group in discussion. Their response? Silence. No one said a word, but their eyes darted back and forth, looking at one another. Who would talk first? That behavior was familiar to me, too, so I took a somewhat different approach.

"Here are some ideas," I said. "We could play games, make cookies, go on a scavenger hunt, go swimming—" and before I could finish my list of options, they all started talking at once, calling out their preferences.

"Okay! One at a time." Quickly as I could, I wrote on the chart to capture their ideas on paper.

So what do you get when you put a retired corporate executive in a room alone with four grandchildren and a flip chart? That's right: Camp Grandma was a hit from day one. It was to become an ongoing experience that right from the beginning allowed me to connect with my grandchildren in unexpected ways that positively impact us all. Through our activities, I would realize years later, we began building a generational bridge over which I could transfer skills to benefit their lives for years to come—and they would do the same for me.

Of course, it didn't happen all at once. At first, I thought of myself as a babysitter. But that quickly changed. I found myself wanting more than to merely supervise. I wanted to know my grandkids and for them to know me. I wanted to participate in activities with them to fully engage in our time together. That meant that I needed to come up with activities that I, too, would enjoy. In this role, I was proactive and drew from the broader platform of my working experience to create ideas for my time with them. With Camp Grandma, I changed my mind-set.

BUILDING A LASTING BOND

My intention for Camp Grandma started to evolve that first summer. My time with them went deeper than babysitting. And it was more than intergenerational bonding I foresaw. I wanted to establish a structure where my four grandkids could come together and through shared experiences truly learn about each other and maybe more about themselves. I hoped to offer them enough time to establish relationships between themselves based on trust, understanding, and acceptance. It's hard to do that when the only time they see each other is when the families are together briefly for holidays or birthday parties. But consistently being together on a regular basis—that kind of time can build a lasting bond.

I began to see whom I had before me: four different children, different in age, different in disposition, different in temperament. Though two of the parents are brother and sister (my children), my grandchildren had been raised in different households with different priorities and interests. I imagined Camp Grandma could provide a form of diversity training for them, unlike their chosen circle of friends or peer group. I started to recognize the five-year age difference between the oldest and the youngest as a potential learning opportunity. I wondered how many things a grandparent could expose them to that most parents don't have time for because they often run out of gas in the process of covering all their other responsibilities.

Again, drawing on my background as a business executive, I found myself bringing to the table core leadership values I'd practiced throughout my work life with success. I noticed the kids were becoming familiar with such skills like working collaboratively, learning to value others' ideas, planning time with intention—all through play—and they were having fun doing it. I also realized they were learning people skills that would help them succeed at whatever they ultimately chose to do. Meanwhile, I was understanding that these were personal skills that factor not only into professional success but also into overall happiness.

CHAPTER TWO:

GRANDPARENTING 2.0

Something magical happened as I spent time and got to know my grandchildren. I didn't see them as just other kids, and I didn't feel the same way about them as I did my own children. I encountered a whole new experience. It was different—way different for me and totally unexpected. I came to appreciate the multigenerational distance between us as an actual benefit. It gave me perspective.

I began to see them, really see them, from this new and unique vantage point. I saw their natural gifts and their potential. I saw their innocence and faith in a world that they expected to be fair and just. They were earnest and trusting. They so wanted to be seen and recognized for who they were—and to find their place and to know they mattered.

And they saw me too. With them I was not fading out of the picture as I was in an American culture so obsessed with youth. My grandchildren regarded me for who I was, at the moment, in the moment. They didn't give a hoot what my GPA was in school, what titles I'd achieved in my work life, or what kind of car I drove (as long as it had all the newest bells and whistles!). We enjoyed the human connection without judgment or expectation. We were who we were, and we found joy in discovering what the other had to offer. They reminded me of things I knew as a kid but had forgotten, and I showed them what it was like to be old, having survived this thing called life. We traded wisdoms and exchanged energy. We were there for each other, mutually sharing, learning, growing, and finding purpose through our match.

THE GRANDPARENT STEREOTYPE

I became so engaged in experiencing this amazing connection with the kids that I was caught off guard one day at a social gathering when I shared what I was doing with my life. I recalled a few years earlier, as retirement approached, how friends I'd known for years had frequently asked, "What will you do next?" Initially, my answer had been, "Business coaching and consulting," to which the response was always very encouraging and complimentary. People were impressed and interested, continuing the conversation with questions like "Who will you coach?" and "What kind of consulting will you do?" It was obvious that people viewed these pursuits as important.

By contrast, when I shared at this social gathering that I was spending the summer with my grandchildren, I received a different response entirely. A few people offered up a weak smile: A few others didn't quite know where to take the conversation from there. "Taking care of your grandchildren? Oh, how nice . . . They're lucky to have you . . ." they said, their voices and interest trailing off. There was definitely something off there. Didn't they see I was the lucky one? I have to admit that the lackluster response among some of my peers threw me off at first. But the more I shared, and the more it happened, the more it got me thinking.

Clearly, being a grandparent was not a role that drew the oohs and ahhs my big corporate title once did. But I could deal with that personally. What disturbed me more was to realize how undervalued grandparenting is culturally. What is the societal perception of grandparenting? How is it valued? What impact does the role of grandparent have on our culture, and on kids? How do people feel about it? In business, answering these questions leads us to better understand what we call "the brand." So analyzing this with my corporate hat on, I couldn't help but ask myself, *What is the brand of the grandparent in our society?*

Let's face it, becoming a grandparent just happens to us. We have no say in the matter. Maybe since we don't plan and prepare, study and save, for the event in any meaningful way, the persona lacks the prestige and authority it deserves. Am I wrong to get the sense that the general perception of grandparenting is that it's a provincial and rather mundane avocation?

What comes to mind when you hear the word "grandparent"? Gray hair? Round belly, maybe? Glasses, wrinkles? Clearly there's a physical image attached, one shared with old age in general that includes physical limitations such as aching backs, bad knees, and poor stamina. What is the stereotype you see? Someone past their prime, moving with diminished energy, gardening, baking cookies, or reading? Activities with their grandchildren would tend to reflect these slow-paced activities, along with engaging in child-based interests like crafts, coloring, hide-and-seek, and so forth.

Conversely, in this twenty-first century, you will certainly meet the "anti-grandparent," mature and retired baby boomers determined to maintain the activities, friends, and interests of their younger years to prove they're not getting old. You may see them skydiving, hiking the Himalayas, or finding other ways to defy old age. They greatly value their independence, maximizing life after their children have left the home!

Clearly, the role of the grandparent today is not easily defined and fits no cookie cutter description. In fact, I recently learned that the average age people become grandparents is forty-eight! I couldn't believe it. So there's no pinning down what makes an average grandparent, and just because someone is more or less active doesn't make them a more or less engaged grandparent. Time available— especially a lack of time—can have a lot to do with how involved grandparents will be in their grandchildren's lives. Some grandparents are still fully immersed in their careers, leaving less time to refocus on family and grandchildren.

Health concerns can limit the time grandparents spend with their grandchildren, as can the distance they live from their grandchildren.

Whatever the reasons, I seldom hear grandparents declare they've made their grandchildren the focus of their senior years. Clearly, the *brand* of grandparent lacks the commercial cache to attract interest and attention or to gain a high regard in our society today. I've identified a few reasons why this might be.

Grandparenting Is Unpaid Work

Most grandparents donate their time and don't put a price tag on the hours they spend with their grandchildren. Does that make this investment of time viewed as less valuable? Is the amount of money we earn the determining factor that defines our status? The higher the paycheck, the greater the prestige? Does our society place too great a premium on salaries and titles rather than value added?

Most grandparents who care for their grandchildren do so without fanfare or recognition. They operate on a mere thank-you and a loving hug. They cherish the deeper rewards they gain through the untold pleasures and joys of knowing their grandchildren and being part of their lives. Why this isn't generally regarded as important as a six-figure paycheck beats me. Americans clearly hold dear what we pay for. Do some of us *not* see value if a price tag is not attached? I wonder.

Our Contributions Aren't as Valued as They Once Were

Historically, a major benefit of three generations being alive at the same time was the preservation of information. Clearly, this advantage is less relevant today. We have multiple avenues for accessing information at our fingertips. Yet information about heritage and stories reflecting family values and experiences are often lost without a grandparent's involvement. Certainly, there are popular websites that will trace your lineage or ancestry, but they can only provide treetop information. Memories are not stored in any independent computer data system.

Grandparents can provide continuity and a sense of family tradition to a child's life. They can instill respect and a positive attitude for other ages and stages of life. Coming from a different time and place, separate generations share their values and speak with a different tone. This layering of values of one generation onto another creates the foundation for a more multifaceted, well-rounded person. It can forge the framework and boundaries within which children thrive. Just the sheer information transfer from the old to the young provides a significant evolutionary advantage.

Like a tree, with deep roots, we gain a stable anchor or foundation that secures us through adversity. With family, you can create deep connections. Knowing and understanding where you come from helps in visualizing where you're going. Family can help ground you by offering a sense of place and permanence in the world. It's a sad commentary if this contribution is overlooked.

Job Expectations Are Unclear

Clearly, a grandparent lacks a well-defined job description. But isn't that the beauty of it? There aren't expectations of what one should or must do. This enabled me to immediately find what I love most about the role of Grandma: that it is mine to create and develop. I can invest my time and energy in what I believe to be most important. But I can see where this could be a challenge as well. Without clear expectations, some may not know where to start. With ambiguous roles and the fast-paced changes taking place almost daily in our society, it is hard to know just where a grandparent can fit in.

That took me to thinking about my own grandparents, about whom I have many memories, all of them good. And that was the biggest disconnect of all. Don't most people remember their grandparents fondly? And if they do, how can they possibly have a lackluster response to the role of the grandparent? I understand that maybe some people weren't close to their grandparents or never knew them. But even without that personal interaction, I'm not sure that explains those who undervalue the relationship.

I began to realize that I was one of a long line of grandparents, each of us setting the course for the new generation. In becoming a grandmother, I already had role models for the job, and they lived within me as memories of my own special grandparents—especially my grandmothers.

CHAPTER THREE:

STANDING ON THEIR SHOULDERS

L ooking back from the perspective of adulthood, I began to realize the effect my grandmothers had on me.

My grandmothers couldn't have been more different, and I received an early education in diversity from knowing them. They lived three thousand miles apart, came from different cultures, and spoke different languages.

Immigrants from Italy, my father's parents both arrived in America through Ellis Island but not together. Grandfather Phillippo Pasquarelli, born near Rome but raised in Naples, was just seventeen years old and alone when he decided to stow away on a ship to America to start a new life in 1903. He was barely alive when he docked in New York Harbor, and since he was without a passport or papers (hence, the term "WOP"), US officials were going to send him back to Italy on the next ship. Fortunately, a nurse working in the hospital on the island intervened. Fearing he wouldn't survive the voyage back, she took care of him until he was well enough to venture out on his own. My grandmother, Maria Gallo, his future wife, was sixteen when she came to America ten years later. Maria left Italy to escape a planned marriage. She boarded an Italian vessel to New York Harbor, traveling third class (water level). Her ticket cost sixty dollars, which was paid by her older sister, already living in Riverside, Connecticut.

My grandparents met at a neighborhood christening party not far from where Maria lived. Phillippo was working on the road crew constructing the Boston Post Road (now Route 1 from Boston to New York City), and he was asked to play his button accordion at the event. When he saw Maria, it was love at first sight. They were married seventy years.

Whenever we visited them in Connecticut, my grandmother was in the kitchen and my grandfather in his garden. Family was central to their lives, and everything revolved around the kitchen table. She was an unsophisticated yet wonderful cook, and she wasn't happy unless she was feeding you—homemade everything, of course. "Mangia, mangia" was an early Italian phrase I learned spending time at their house.

My father was one of their eight children, and except for him and another son who moved out West, all settled relatively close to the family homestead to raise their families. When the Connecticut clan got together (which was at the very least every Sunday for spaghetti), there was frequently music, singing, and dancing, with my grandfather playing his accordion and my grandmother playing along with her tambourine and castanets.

I was raised in California, where my mother was born. Her parents were refined, reserved, and well educated. Their heritage was English, Irish, Swiss, and Pennsylvania Dutch, and they could trace their roots in America back to 1726. Her parents met in high school and later married while attending the University of California, Berkeley. My maternal grandmother, Goldie Shellenberger, had been valedictorian of her high school and graduated from Berkeley in 1910, which is very impressive when you consider the lack of opportunity for women at that time (and for many years after).

My grandfather, Charles Cunningham, was later appointed to the diplomatic service and served as commercial attaché for the embassy of the United States (equivalent today to an ambassador). This gave my grandparents the opportunity to experience the world, living first in the Philippines and later in Spain, Mexico, and Peru. They dined with kings, entertained the highest dignitaries, and were accorded all the honors given to diplomats.

I never knew my grandfather Charles as he died before I was born, but I was close to my maternal grandmother, Goldie, and share much of her sensibility. I decorate my home much like hers, with fine antiques and treasures from around the world. I like to collect, as she did, beautiful teacups, hand-painted plates, sterling silver spoons, and special artifacts representative of diverse cultures. I love to entertain, I love learning, and I love to travel to exotic places, three of her favorite pastimes.

This nana embraced a wide range of interests and relished seeking new experiences. I learned so much from her. She taught me to play bridge and canasta. (I love playing cards!) Oh, and chocolate! Gotta love a grandmother who hides Hershey bars in her lingerie drawer for her granddaughter to find. And there was something else about her I found fascinating—her curious mind. For while she was the wife of a diplomat and held formal parties for as many as eighty-five people at a time, she also had her secret passions for astrology and tarot cards. I was intrigued by her breadth of interests and abilities: some formal and so proper, others more playful and fanciful. It was fun for me to discover her different sides.

When my parents married, it must have been like two different worlds uniting—or colliding, as it turned out. Yet I was the recipient of the best of both of those worlds. From my nana back east, I came to appreciate family and the value of keeping it together. She was a strong woman and demonstrated, through selfless giving, the role of caretaker and problem solver, providing a safe harbor for all under her wing.

From Goldie, my nana in Los Angeles, I learned a sense of propriety and independence along with a fearless can-do attitude. She didn't need the feminist movement to prove a woman could make her own way. She wrote her own valedictory speech in high school called "The Power of the Individual" in 1905. She was way ahead of her time.

I am a combination of both my grandmothers. I noticed years ago that I am more like my grandmothers than I am either my mother or father, which was a remarkable insight. I wondered if there might be a pattern here, as I have the impression that characteristics tend to skip generations. My husband is much like his grandfather, and my daughter shares much in common with my mother. It will be fun to see if any of my grandchildren take after me.

I realize now, as a grandmother, that in their own distinct ways, my grandmothers empowered me to be the person I am today. They were both strong women and ignited in me my passion for family and love of continuous learning, along with the strong core values of faith, fortitude, loyalty, self-reliance, and always doing my best. I learned from their examples how to overcome obstacles, and they taught me to embrace life with gratitude, which I know is the basis of my happiness. I also learned that it doesn't hurt to believe in a little magic now and then either.

PART 2.
CAMP GRANDMA

Camp Grandma is officially open

CHAPTER FOUR:

A CORPORATE RETREAT
FOR KIDS

I should have seen it coming when I started with the flip chart. But it was only much later that I realized what we had in the making. You could say that Camp Grandma evolved to resemble a child's version of a corporate retreat. Okay, I know that may sound weird, and I never consciously thought of it that way in the beginning. It's just that as it evolved, I started bringing more of my work-life expertise into our day-to-day doings.

In the adult world, when done right, corporate retreats are great escapes from the everyday world and are known for reenergizing participants through training and collaboration. They usually start with setting goals and lofty expectations (like writing mission statements or discussing branding). Then, through presentations and team exercises, they add fun and activity, all in an effort to educate and inspire the participants. These sessions can be powerful. One reason they are so effective is because you're not working alone but collaboratively in teams, which can be more rewarding than working independently. They also provide an open environment, welcoming of ideas and questions. This can promote stimulating communication through which to develop creative ideas, a sharing that contributes to a sense of belonging—just what we wanted to accomplish at Camp Grandma.

So I tailored the children's version to fit our needs. We began our sessions each morning around an easel. I included presentations along with activities and exercises encompassing the key elements of communication, goal setting, learning, and, of course, fun! Much like an old one-room schoolhouse, I liked that we had a mixed-age setting. The younger ones emulated the older ones and saw them as role models, and the older ones gained confidence by helping the younger ones (even if they didn't know it). Everyone gained something!

THE PARTICIPANTS

Before I tell you about a typical day at Camp Grandma, let me introduce you to my grandchildren. Jack and Katie are my daughter's children, and Jake and Lauren are my son's.

Jack is the oldest, with a full head of thick, sandy brown hair, which I often remind him to comb. He sometimes complains about being the oldest, feeling as if it were a burden.

He thinks that too much is expected of him, and he feels the pressure. Since I, too, am the oldest in my family, I try to help him see the advantages of the position. I remind him that Mom and Dad count on him because they know they can. I tell him, "It's cool to be the oldest, Jack. You get to be in charge!" I'm not sure I have fully convinced him yet, but as he gets older I can see him developing into a highly responsible, protective, and loyal young man.

Jack often enters with his hands in his pockets and a rather disinterested look on his face. "Hi, Grandma," he says as he comes over to give me a hug. I know Jack—he tends to be a homebody and resists anything new until he tries it and surprises himself by liking the new experience.

Katie comes in with a smile accompanying her hug. She always looks forward to the day and a chance to play with her cousin Lauren. Katie is three years younger than her brother, Jack, tall for her age, and slender with long brown hair, the color of her mother's at her age. She is an A student, she's well behaved and cooperative, and she wants people around her to be happy. I call her the Peacekeeper. Rather delicate in nature, she tends to be quiet and is able to occupy herself for hours. Katie is meticulous and patiently takes the time she needs to complete any task with care (though she may need prompting to finish).

She loves to sing, and onstage, Katie blooms into quite the performer, animated, forceful, and holding back nothing from her part. It is remarkable how she transforms from the rather shy and reserved little girl we all know.

Jake and Lauren enthusiastically run up the stairs when they arrive. Jake always drops off his book bag on the counter in the kitchen. He never goes anywhere without ten or fifteen books in his large canvas bag.

Jake is without a doubt his own man. He is the second oldest (two years younger than Jack, though almost as tall), and I marvel at his interests. He can focus intently without distraction. Anything about outer space and the planets continues to be a favorite, but as he's gotten older, he's taken an interest in art and has been copying the masters. He'd rather go to a museum than an amusement park.

His eyeglasses give him the appearance of an academic, in keeping with his more intellectual pursuits. He has an extraordinary memory for what matters to him. He once wrote a timeline of the world, with it ending the day NASA lost its funding. He has a keen sense of place and is deliberate in his actions.

Lauren is the youngest of the group, which, like being the oldest, is cause for complaint. She, too, is tall for her age, with light brown hair. Lauren is outgoing, sometimes silly (taking after her dad), and good-natured. She likes to sing and dance and makes funny videos for her cousins. She is the grandchild with whom I have spent the most time since I had just retired when she was born.

Lauren is easy to be with, maybe because of the time we have spent together or because she is the grandchild most like me. We have a lot in common. She is a people pleaser and a problem solver, makes friends easily, and is a natural caretaker. More than just bright, she is wise beyond her years, as well as a good planner and organizer. I often remark that she is nine going on thirty.

THE AGENDA

The four grandchildren are dropped off at my home by their parents, usually by 8:30 a.m. They call the house I live in "Granada," which is the name of the street where I reside. Once all the kids arrive, Camp Grandma begins.

"Hey, Grandma, guess what?" Lauren asked one day when she was around seven, having spent two summers at Camp Grandma by that point in her young life.

"What, dear?"

"I made the agenda for Camp Grandma today!" Lauren proudly announced as she waved the paper in her hand. She already well knew that at Camp Grandma we begin each day with an agenda.

The agenda not only gives structure to their day but also sets goals and expectations. It gives voice to what they will be doing and accomplishing. And this is another way in which Camp Grandma is like a corporate retreat. Planning is important, and it's never too early to start. It's about more than just setting priorities. It's about having an ongoing process that keeps people on track and focused on what they want to accomplish—no matter how old they are. I want my grandkids to begin thinking about how they can take charge of their days, their years, and their lives.

"Okay, everyone," I announced, "let's begin our time together today. Please meet me at the table."

"I want to sit next to Katie," Lauren said, rushing to the table to grab a seat and show Katie her chair. Jake brought along his pen and paper to continue with his writing. Jack thoughtfully brought over an extra chair from my desk so we'd all have a seat.

We gathered around my kitchen table. We call this Table Time—almost always the first item on the agenda. Table time is when we focus on filling in plans for the other categories of the agenda, which fall under the headings Presentations, Things to Learn, and Activity Time. This is also a time to practice mindfulness. This involves focusing on the present moment and being aware of thoughts, feelings, and experiences. It means being accepting; it's nonjudgmental. It has to do with paying attention so that whatever we do or say has purpose. And at Camp Grandma we've always made choices based on those observations, which means it's important that we remain flexible. We don't set specific time frames in our agenda because a plan should always leave room for the unexpected, which will happen whether it's good or bad (an obstacle). As in the corporate world, a plan should not squash the creativity and pleasure that come from that magical chemistry of spontaneity and focus, a blend that can create some of the best ideas in the world. It's the same at Camp Grandma.

Here's a typical agenda:

1. Table Time. I start with some suggestions, usually based on activities I have prepared for the day or ingredients I've purchased for a special recipe. I try to give the kids options and choices. They then discuss and agree together on what they want to do. This is where we also set some general time frames.

2. Presentations. This is our time for show and tell (see chapter 5).

3. Things to Learn. I suggest a number of possibilities, including manners/etiquette, write your résumé, candle making, and meet your ancestors.

4. Activity Time. This may include swimming, bowling, performing a play, doing crafts, baking/cooking, making Christmas presents, going on a treasure hunt, and more. The kids decide on the particular activities we'll do, and then we always add some free time for whatever fun thing they feel like doing.

I encourage you to adapt the above agenda as needed to suit your needs and those of your grandchildren.

ROUND-TABLE DISCUSSION

The kids decide who will facilitate that day's discussion. The facilitator is the one who writes the agenda on the easel and leads the discussion on suggestions. I try to keep quiet, but being a Type A personality, I often can't help but throw in a comment or two. The ideas for the day start streaming in. Frequently, Lauren comes in with an agenda she has already written. Although the youngest, she's the planner in the bunch. We inevitably incorporate many of her ideas into our day, but we don't finalize our plan until all opinions are heard and considered.

When I first introduced the concept of planning together as a team, we started with a pretty simple outline. Our agenda included group time at the table, a structured activity, and social time. The agenda was basically used to organize our day together, but the kids enjoyed setting the agenda and wanted to give more input. As I saw them standing in front of the flip chart, I recalled the countless times I was part of a training session at work and it dawned on me: the "core competencies" that enhance your experience in the workplace have to start somewhere, so why not here?

It took off from there. One activity led to an idea for another. Eventually we were giving presentations, writing résumés, and doing strategic planning and team building exercises—all elements of a typical corporate retreat. As my grandchildren got older, they provided the content, and we modified it per their direction, along with my input. All I ask is that they come prepared with a presentation to make to the group. The rest of the day is theirs to create.

SET GOALS, BUT BE FLEXIBLE

Although we like to structure our days so we can accomplish our goals, we don't ever want to be too rigid at the expense of creative play. We adults may be guilty of overplanning or overworking our days, potentially missing opportunities that unexpectedly come our way. We might all do better to take the lead from kids. Be prepared to have fun at a moment's notice.

So create a plan. And be courageous to modify it or even throw it out if something better presents itself. Because, even with the best of intentions, things can go awry or an unexpected opportunity may surface, and we all need to learn to be flexible and go with the punches when need be. This, too, can be a good learning experience.

One afternoon at Camp Grandma when we were all together, I unpacked a shipping box. Inside was a white cardboard cutout, like a picture frame. Jack grabbed it and held it up to his face and started making funny faces.

"Take a picture, Grandma!" he exclaimed. Next thing I knew, they were all asking for turns (me included).

"Me next!"

"I want a turn."

I ran and got my camera to capture this spontaneous and delightful moment. They had the best time. And it wasn't even on the agenda!

ACTIVITY: GOAL SETTING

Following are some ideas for teaching kids about goal setting. Goal setting is the process of identifying something you want to accomplish and creating a plan to do it. Whether you set a short-term goal (I'm going to mow and edge the lawn this weekend) or a long-term goal (I want to earn my master's degree), committing to the process ensures you reach your goal and get the job done.

What Kids Will Learn

- How to focus on what they desire
- How to take control of their life and choose the direction they want to go
- How to make a commitment
- How to motivate themselves to get something they want

- How to feel a sense of accomplishment and self-confidence from the rewards of their efforts

What You Need

- A notebook
- A pencil or pen

What You'll Do

1. Sit down with your grandchildren and ask them to tell you something they would like to accomplish (maybe get a part in the school play, an A in English, or an after-school job).

2. Ask them to write it down. Writing it down is critical since research shows that the people who write down their goals achieve a lot more success than those who don't.

3. Now apply the SMART goal-setting process by asking and discussing the following:

> **S—Specific:** Is the goal clear and well-defined?
> **M—Measurable:** Does it include dates or amounts so you can measure success?
> **A—Attainable:** Is this goal actually achievable?
> **R—Realistic:** Is it consistent with your direction in life?
> **T—Time-Bound:** Does it have a deadline or a period in which to complete it?

For instance, instead of saying "My goal is to start improving the environment," a better goal statement would be "Because I care about our planet, my goal is to start collecting recyclables, one bag a month."

4. After they have stated their goal, create a plan of action. Fill in with steps necessary to reach the goal. If they follow the SMART goals criteria, they have a great start on their plan since it already includes the objective, measurement, and time frame. Now they just need to put it in motion.

Time Required

Start with about one hour. More than that and your grandchildren will tire. Then follow up periodically to check on their progress. How often will depend on whether it is a short- or long-term goal.

Tips

- You can begin with educational, family, and physical goals and then advance to include career, spiritual, financial, and social and personal development goals.
- Don't forget to celebrate! That's part of the fun and keeps kids motivated to achieve their next goal!
- You can participate right along with your grandchildren and set a goal for yourself. You can support and cheer each other on so that you can all achieve your goals.

Painting birdhouses

CHAPTER FIVE:

SPEAKING UP

"What's going on in here?" I asked as I entered the kitchen one day that first summer at Camp Grandma. I heard the girls squabbling over the pointer we used with the flip chart.

"I want a turn to use it!"

"Not now, I'm using it!"

"But I want to do the talking, and I need the pointer."

"But I'm not done with it yet!"

Apparently standing in front of the flip chart to lead a discussion had become a popular activity. Hmm, this gave me another idea. They had something they wanted to say (don't we all?), so maybe they needed a platform on which to do it.

THE IMPORTANCE OF COMMUNICATION

My years in business had underscored the value of good communication skills. Nothing is more essential in life, work, or relationships. A good friend of mine used to say you can never communicate enough. Your ability to communicate thoughts in a clear and succinct manner is critical if you want to convey information or feelings and avoid misunderstanding and frustration. Understanding how to use the power of words can be a transformational skill. Words matter. They can influence or destroy, hurt or heal. They can also be fun to play around with at Camp Grandma, I was now discovering.

"Okay," I intervened. "I want to hear what you have to say, both of you. And the boys may want to hear too. So let's take turns, and you can each have a chance to talk to all of us. Yes, with the pointer. Jake, Jack, please join us at the table."

Even in its earliest days, Camp Grandma benefitted from my giving it a structure. Having named it seemed to ramp it up a notch in value and to mandate a modicum of focus and ritual. You do get the most value out of something by giving it a structure aligned with your intentions. I wanted what every parent, grand or otherwise, wants for the generations coming after them—to live a good life—so if my experience and mentoring could be of help in that, I was sure going to try.

Once they were all sitting (or squirming) around the table, I began. "When I was in elementary school we used to speak in front of the class about something we wanted to share. We called this show and tell. Have you ever done that?" They nodded their heads but appeared to be skeptical of where this was leading. "I always liked it as a child in class, and I frequently did a form of it in my adult career too. Grown-ups call it giving presentations."

And so began our exercise in giving presentations to each other and learning the skills required to be good at it. I learned from my work life that acquiring the skill set of public speaking can be a game changer. It's a powerful tool that improves your ability to communicate and builds self-confidence. If you are good at it and comfortable on your feet, it can launch your career, and for kids it can help them better communicate in class and on the playground. You never know when you might be asked to give a speech, accept an award, or express yourself in front of a group of people. Learning to speak in front of an audience served me well in my career, as I was often asked to present, sell, or promote when in front of colleagues and clients. It occurred to me that the experience would be good for my grandchildren and give them a head start.

As a side note, let's just acknowledge that most adults regard speaking in front of an audience with dread. (Fortunately, I am not one of them, although I do have the occasional butterflies in my stomach.) My observations have led me to believe that children are not born with that particular problem. It's easy for them to speak up, provided they are comfortable in their surroundings.

ALL TYPES OF PRESENTATIONS

Giving presentations would soon become a mainstay. We never knew what anyone would choose to discuss, but Jake always had a special surprise for us, like the time he got up from his chair and started emptying his pockets.

"Hi, I'm Jake," he started. "I'm going to do a magnet presentation. Here is my demonstration." Out came a paperclip, a single jingle bell, a curled wire spring, a binder clip, and a magnet. He proceeded to demonstrate the power of the magnet on each of the other objects. "That was my magnet demonstration," he concluded, and he sat down. He is a man of few words.

We started including presentations at every Camp Grandma. I always ask that they come prepared. Everyone has to contribute, but the way they do it is entirely up to them. Maybe they share a story, a demonstration, a favorite toy, a poem. Our presentations at Camp Grandma aren't all that formal—we always have fun! But the one formality all must respect is whose turn it is to speak. This, I'm hoping, will encourage them as adults to speak up if they have something to say and afford the courtesy to others to have their say, good qualities of a citizen in a free democracy.

Sometimes the presentations have entailed being introduced to favorite stuffed toys (Tum Tum the tiger has had center stage at least sixteen times) or we hear about a scouting adventure or a school field trip or a recent vacation.

Recently returned from a visit to Boston when she was around eight years old, Lauren stood up at the table, introduced herself, and presented a purple drawing and note to

Katie. She read, "Hi, Katie. I would do anything for you and know you've never been to Boston. You wanna go there, it's amazing! So I'm bringing Boston to you and with your best color, purple! Be happy all the time, love and peace, this is from Boston, Lauren."

Sometimes I give the kids a topic to read about and discuss. One day I told them, "Please come prepared next time to either read a famous poem or read a poem you wrote." They didn't blink. A poem? Yup!

The next time they came to Granada for Camp Grandma, Lauren had ready a poem she wrote about Halloween.

Halloween's a spooky night
where you hang jack-o'-lanterns' light.
Come with me, there's so much to see.
Boo for you, Halloween!

Not exactly iambic pentameter, but clever enough for a seven-year-old.

Jake, who was ten at the time, started right in with "Tyger, Tyger, burning bright / In the forests of the night. . . ." He finished after reciting two complete stanzas by William Blake.

Sometimes we hear a song.

One day, all of a sudden Jack got up, introduced himself, and started singing, "This is the pizza, pizza, pizza song, sounds like the pizza, pizza, pizza song." Before long, all four kids were up and dancing, singing the pizza song. It was crazy and wild, arms flinging, hair flying, and you could barely hear the words through the giggling and laughing. I couldn't resist joining in the fun—why not, I needed the exercise. "This is the pizza, pizza, pizza song. . . ."

Not too long after we started giving presentations regularly, I attended a music recital for Jack and Katie. Out of about twenty children of varying ages asked to introduce themselves and their music, they were the only two who spoke clearly into the microphone and looked out at the audience. Eye to eye. I was proud of them and glad to think that their speaking in front of cousins at Camp Grandma had taken the sting out of one of the most commonly feared things in life. I hope so.

At Mother's Day dinner at my home one year, with all the family sitting around the table, Jake educated us about China, a topic he had recently studied in school. My son later remarked to me how surprised he was that Jake had carried the conversation, taking the lead in the discussion. I wasn't surprised at all. Dad has never been to Camp Grandma to see how comfortable Jake is speaking in front of his cousins. That they all could be there to witness it was a bonus.

Seeing firsthand how beneficial these speaking skills were for my grandkids led me to build in other skill sets that too often only get learned in the workplace, far too late in my opinion. Combining learning with play is the ticket. Why not help them learn with intention? I started keeping a journal of what the kids were learning from Camp Grandma and what I was learning from them. This gave me ideas for future activities and ways to build other skills into the structure.

With all this learning and play, the kids weren't the only ones becoming more and more engaged; I was too. In fact, I felt the onset of total engagement, a feeling that had infused my career and now seemed to be catching on to my retirement. Even I was surprised when I realized how much time I spent with my grandchildren, and I was happy to conclude that it was exactly how I wanted it to be. I was all in.

If you're working on a presentation, here are some ideas to keep in mind.

KEY ELEMENTS OF A GOOD PRESENTATION

1. Have something worth saying. Know your purpose. (Do you want your audience to learn something? Feel something? Do something?) Whether you are rallying your team to victory as a cheerleader (as I did in school) or standing in front of an audience of business leaders discussing new strategies (as I did on many occasions), feeling your message to be important, or useful to others, is critical. You, of all people, need to know what that message is to communicate it clearly.

2. Be prepared. Know your audience and speak so they understand you, not too fast or slow, loud or soft. Check out the room or location where you will be presenting before your talk and get comfortable with the size and amenities, like lighting, seating arrangement, and technology (audiovisual). Whenever possible beforehand, I practiced my presentation in the room where I would be speaking.

Honor your audience with time limits. Start on time and don't exceed your allotted time period. Then tell them what you're going to tell them, tell them, and then tell them what you told them!

3. Dress the part. "I see by your outfit that you are a cowboy." There's something to those lyrics to an old song. If a costume makes you feel more the part, then get in it. In other words, dress appropriately. I liked to dress one notch nicer than my audience, out of respect.

4. Be you. Be sincere. Remember to breathe. Make eye contact, enunciate, gesture, and try to act like you are enjoying yourself. More often than not, people will take their cues about how to react to you from you. Be comfortable and confident knowing you are prepared and have something worth sharing with the group.

I remember a time I was asked to speak to a large group of business leaders at a community event, an economic development conference I think. I was on stage and the audiovisual equipment failed, so I couldn't refer to my overhead presentation notes. Yikes! Though I felt like panicking, instead I explained the situation and asked the audience for their patience and understanding. Then I proceeded to talk to them in a more informal, casual way, making the points but inviting their participation through questions and answers even more than usual. It turned out to be a success, interactive and educational for everybody, including me. I learned that people in an audience tend to want you to do well, and they'll help you if you let them.

ACTIVITY: PUBLIC SPEAKING

Being able to speak comfortably and confidently in front of an audience is a communication skill that can help you both personally and professionally. Many people have a phobia of public speaking, so learning early in life how to overcome the fear of speaking in front of others gives your grandchildren a head start in the world. It can strongly impact how they view themselves and how they develop and succeed in school and beyond.

What Kids Will Learn

- To build self-confidence in their ability to express themselves (whether with a small group of friends or in front of a crowd)
- To plan ahead by thinking through what they want to say
- To grow interpersonal and social skills
- The connection between self-esteem and believing they have something worth saying

What You Need

Time and patience. I have found with my own grandchildren, some are more excited to speak in front of each other, while others need to be prompted. Typically, most kids want to be heard. They have something to say and need adults who will take the time to be good listeners. This is where you come in.

With older children, you might want to use a flip chart or chalkboard so they can learn to outline what they have to say and then reference their notes as prompts.

What You'll Do

1. With young children, you can start by encouraging your grandchildren to engage in conversation when the family is together. Or you might ask them to describe to you a favorite game or vacation experience.

2. When they are telling you a story, ask them, "What happens next?" or "What did you do then?"

3. Your main role is to start the ball rolling. Identify opportunities to speak publicly in front of others and encourage them.

4. Engage their whole family in skits, songs, and other entertainment when you are all together for holidays (as my friends the Smiths do!). This is a fun way to include the adults along with the children.

Once your grandchild is old enough, say six or seven years old, you can begin by asking them for a show and tell presentation as we did at Camp Grandma, and build from there. They could present in front of you or include Mom or Dad and maybe cousins or friends. Work with them behind the scenes by teaching them the basics in preparation and delivery. Ask that they think first about their audience and choose a topic that would be of interest to them all. When their turn comes, ask them to stand up and introduce themselves and the topic of their presentation. Help them with the physical elements: posture, eye contact, and use of their voice so all in the room can hear.

Time Required

Clearly this will vary, depending on the age and interest of your grandchild. It could be as little as ten minutes if you are asking about a favorite toy or more than an hour if he or she is performing.

Tips

- Encourage your grandchild to tell their audience what they are going to talk about, talk about it, and then tell them what they said. It's a good habit to get into when you want to get your point across. A preview tells the audience where they are going so they can comprehend it once they are there, and a review reinforces the message.

- Afterward discuss how things went, how they could be better, and how what you did reflected the *key elements* of a good presentation. This is a perfect time to test their listening skills, since a good listener knows how to restate the message back to the sender or ask questions for clarity, all of which can enhance the effectiveness of good communication.

- If you don't live near your grandchildren and aren't with them in person, you can still help them with public speaking if you Skype together. Ask them to tell you stories or share their interests. This can give them some of the same public speaking experience, even if it's only between the two of you.

Speaking up!

CHAPTER SIX:

ARE YOU LISTENING?

I have learned that listening is as important, if not more important, than talking. Many believe that the load of good communication is on the listener, not the speaker. Poor listening skills are actually more common than poor speaking skills. The ability to accurately receive and interpret information requires focus. A good listener pays attention not only to the spoken message but also to tone, body language, and nonverbal cues. It takes concentration as well as openness to fully interpret the meaning of what is being communicated.

Were we ever taught how to listen? I remember in school, when we were taught communication skills, the emphasis was always on delivering, not receiving. Maybe we took a class in public speaking or participated in a

Toastmasters program for our career training, but a class dedicated to listening? I don't think so. There is clearly a challenge in teaching listening, despite its obvious importance in communication. To begin with, how do you really know if someone is listening or not? They may be hearing you, as in perceiving sound, but not listening, which requires paying attention to what is being said. Listening is something you consciously choose to do, and it takes practice.

LISTENING LESSONS

I was delighted that our sessions at Camp Grandma afforded an opportunity for lessons in listening that flowed from speaking. So, as I noticed the relative ease with which the kids got up to give their presentations, it was talking over the presenter and not listening that was my grandkids' problem on that first day of show and tell at Camp Grandma. Paying attention to the speaker was clearly the challenge. I understand that once kids have something to say, they want to say it, often interrupting another speaker. It takes considerable control and patience to learn when it's your turn to talk. I pointed out to them that they have two ears and one mouth—which meant they should listen twice as much as they should speak.

That gave them something to think about, and I resisted mentioning how much adults tend to interrupt, even in the corporate environment, where you'd think they would know better. Maybe it's the fast pace we are all moving at, but I'm noticing more often how people talk over one another, anxious for their turn to share their own thoughts and opinions.

Though presentation skills is a favorite session in training classes and seminars in the working world, I'm glad to learn that many top employers are now providing listening skills training for their employees as well.

At Camp Grandma, we established some ground rules to promote good listening habits. We make sure everyone is quiet and respectful when others speak. And we encourage paying attention, eliminating distractions like playing with toys and mobile devices. I try to model good listening skills myself by asking questions after each presentation or asking the others for input or opinions.

I saw the results of these efforts at Christmas one year. Each child came prepared to discuss Santas from around the world. This was Lauren's idea. She chose Russia and brought along a visual, a small wooden Santa I'd given her from a trip I'd taken there. The boys both chose Germany, by coincidence, and had fun trying to pronounce the name *Weihnachtsmann* (German for "Santa"). Katie chose Italy.

"Hi, I'm Katie," she began, referring to her prepared notes. "The Santa from Italy looks like an old lady riding a broomstick, wearing a black shawl. Her name is Befana. On Christmas Eve she fills the stockings with candy for the good and coal for the bad. She also sweeps the floor before leaving. The people usually leave a cup of wine and some food. That's the story of Befana from Italy."

When Katie was finished, Lauren made the observation, "She sounds like a witch, a good witch."

"Yeah," Jack piped in, "it sounds like they're combining Halloween with Christmas!"

Jake added, "I'm glad we don't."

They all agreed on this point. That they have conversations following the presentations is proof to me that they are listening.

Following instructions is another opportunity for kids to demonstrate their listening skills, or not.

Since listening is a choice, it's impossible to expect them to do everything we ask, at the very moment we ask it. Kids, like adults, prefer to do what they want to do and, if occupied with playing or another activity, might just ignore what you said.

"Jake, time to get out of the pool," I call out.

He glances at me out of the corner of his eye and takes a deep dive. It's easier to turn a deaf ear when you are five feet underwater, right?

I smile, walk over to the edge of the pool, wait for him to come up for air, and say, "You have ten minutes more to swim, then it will be time to get out."

Amazing. Ten minutes later, I see him out of the pool and drying himself off.

I've learned that sometimes kids don't pay attention because they feel no one's paying attention to them.

ACTIVITY: LISTENING

Listening is a skill deserving of more attention. The ability to accurately receive and interpret messages is vital to good communication. The Greek philosopher Epictetus is quoted as saying, "Nature gave us one tongue and two ears so we could hear twice as much as speak." That's a great visual suggesting we should consciously spend less time talking and more time listening.

What Kids Will Learn

- That there is a difference between hearing and listening
- To be patient and wait their turn
- To show respect by being open to other points of view

What You Need

A commitment to make *listening* a priority in your communication.

What You'll Do

1. Start by adopting good listening skills yourself. The best way to teach your grandchildren to be active listeners is to repeatedly show by example.

- Put distracting devices away.
- Make direct eye contact.
- Focus on what is being said.
- Don't interrupt.
- Be attentive to tone, facial expressions, posture, and body language.

2. When together and talking with your grandchildren, be attentive. You may have to ask them questions to get them to open up. Once they do, you can actively engage with good listening techniques.

3. With very young children (three to five years old), notice if they are squirming, jumping up and down, or looking at the floor. What is their body telling you? Are their eyes drifting off in the distance? When they are finished talking, paraphrase to help them along and show you care. "I'm happy to hear about your new stuffed toy. I can see you are excited. Can you tell me more? Did you give it a name?"

4. Make a game of listening. Go on a sound walk with your grandchildren in which they call out all the noises they hear. Or play the copycat game, "Say What I Say," and repeat what the other says.

5. With children ages five to ten, you could play the telephone game. Whisper a sentence around a circle of people, then ask them to pass it on and see what it sounds like when it comes back to you. For instance, whisper the old Turkish saying, "If speaking is silver, then listening is gold." Any saying will do, but this one is worth remembering. The point is to get them engaged with the art of listening.

6. For older grandchildren, start by making them aware of the importance of being active listeners. Let them know they will be better students, learn more about people, and experience less conflict when they learn to listen with intention. There is a difference between hearing (the way we perceive sound) and listening. The latter requires being open to meaning and information. We all want to be valued for who we are and appreciated. Listening is a way to that understanding.

7. Go over the basics of good listening skills. Then practice with them. Engage in conversation. Ask them to paraphrase or restate what they heard so they can demonstrate they were listening. Remind them that listening is not automatic. It takes discipline and effort.

Time Required

All the time you can give.

Tips

- With kids, be aware. They have to want to listen. They're pretty good at tuning out what they don't want to hear, like "Clean your room!" I should point out, this is an activity to improve listening skills, not an activity on minding your parents.

Deep in concentration

CHAPTER SEVEN:

ADDING VALUE

I like the business environment. At its best, it's professional and predictable, with well-defined objectives and goals. You learn to manage budgets and time frames. You dress nicely and work with interesting people, often in teams with a common purpose, leaving your personal agenda at home. Well, at least that's the way it's supposed to work.

When I started caring for my grandchildren, I couldn't help but see the opportunities in the role through my business lens, where by habit I tend to review, analyze, and problem solve in order to be efficient and productive. I wanted to make the most of my time with them and be a positive influence. I realized I had a team again in my four grandchildren. Wow, what an opportunity! I started thinking about what I had learned that might help them on their life's journey. Since I had coached and counseled many adults with topics like understanding your strengths, setting and reaching goals, and developing skills to meet potential, it occurred to me, especially after our success with presentations, that it was certainly not too early to get the kids started with other skills.

All I knew initially was that I wanted to add value to my grandchildren's lives during our time together. Ah yes, I recognize that I'm using another common business term here. Adding value, or value added, is a common business concept that basically describes the enhancement a company gives its product or service to add greater value for its clients or customers. It's about adding features or benefits that go beyond standard expectations. Well, it was second nature for me to want to think about how I could relate this theory to my time with my grandchildren.

FINDING YOUR VALUE

Adding value was one of the first and most valuable lessons I learned in my work life. I remember when I was looking for a job (as a young, single mother), I didn't have a clue where to start. With only three years of college under my belt and a résumé that listed Girl Scout leader and Sunday school teacher, oil painter, and day-care mother, it was no surprise that I didn't have the skills employers were looking for. So I tried to get a job as a waitress. That should have been easy enough considering I had been serving three meals a day to my family for the better part of fourteen years, but apparently not. It appeared I didn't have what they called "experience." Fortunately, I knew someone who owned a local sporting goods store where I was hired as a clerk.

This was my first job outside the home since high school. And my first chance to "add value," though I didn't think of it in those terms at the time. You see, I knew less about sporting goods than I did about waitressing. I never had skied or played soccer and only vaguely remembered how to ride a bike. So I looked around to find something I could do other than bluff my way through a conversation with an actual customer.

The shoe department gave me my mission. It was a disaster. There was nothing in place, shoeboxes were open, and shoes were scattered about. There was always a hunt to find what you were looking for. What a mess! So I jumped in and put the shoes in order by type, color, and size, leaving open spaces so it was clear what to order when inventories were taken. The owner came in when I was finished, took one look at my work, and made me floor supervisor. In less than three weeks I was promoted because I did something unexpected and added value to his store.

Not long after, I started taking business courses at night school. Education is always important but frequently occurs where you least expect it. In talking with an instructor, he suggested I consider a job in sales. Sales? I wasn't interested. I knew it to be a time-honored profession, but I was not attracted to it in the least. Then he said something I will never forget. "You wouldn't feel that way if you were selling something you believed in. What do you believe in?"

I laughed and flippantly remarked, "The Yellow Pages," since I had just looked up a place to take my car for servicing.

"Well then, start there," he suggested.

And so began my career in sales. (Ironically, I did get a job selling advertising in the Yellow Pages!) And sales turned out to be a surprisingly good fit for me. Well, maybe not such a surprise. I liked people and I was a pleaser, so understanding that sales is really only a function of matching customer needs to a product or service was an easy concept for me to grasp. Then I learned the importance of uncovering those needs through good probing (asking questions) and, more importantly, listening for the answers or clues to discover what I could do to meet those needs. Basic stuff.

HANDSHAKES AT CAMP GRANDMA

I would do the same with my grandkids: hear what they needed and provide some basics everybody needs. We started with how to shake hands, since we all need to know how to greet others, right?

At the next Camp Grandma, the kids walked in ready to go.

"Hey, Grandma," Katie said. "What are we doing today?"

"Well, I thought we would learn to shake hands."

"Huh." I could tell they were not at all interested. The rolling eyes up to the ceiling was my first clue.

I knew it didn't seem like a big deal, certainly not to them then, but knowing how to properly shake someone's hand has truly become a forgotten art. Traditionally, it's been the gesture accompanying a formal greeting, closing a deal, offering congratulations, and so on. Coming from the business world, I understood the value of a good handshake. As a first impression it can speak volumes. If your handshake is too limp, it can imply a lack of self-confidence and assertiveness. If too strong, it can seem like a power play or some form of intimidation. It can also mean you are trying to overcompensate for some hidden weakness or insecurity if you're a bone crusher.

Learning how to shake hands properly was something I wanted my grandchildren to know how to do well. Not too firm, not too wimpy, but just right. True, shaking hands is probably more prevalent in the working world, but wouldn't it be just as important to do it right when meeting your teacher or coach? I could see the relevance in this, but also the fun. I was ready for Camp Grandma to have some new programs and activities that would interest not only the kids but me as well. So of course I turned to what I knew and learned in my corporate environment.

I learned the value of showing respect to clients and colleagues by always (yes, always) being truthful when communicating with them, listening to and regarding their input and contribution, and being sincere in my praise and appreciation of their efforts. I valued their time by not being late to meetings and responding to calls within twenty-four hours. I did what I said I would do, and if there was ever a mistake or misunderstanding, I liked to be the first to apologize. Treating people with respect is not only critical in the workplace but also imperative in daily life.

Yet sometimes the best way to teach something is not to load it with platitudes and meaning, but just get to it—put your hands into it, so to speak.

"Let's begin by going over the basics," I cheerfully suggested as I lined up all four of the kids in the family room. "Hold out your right hand. No, not your left, your right hand. This one!"

"Why can't I use my left hand, Grandma?" Lauren asked sweetly.

"Well, a proper handshake is done with your right hand, dear."

"Why?" they all want to know.

"Well, hmm," I stammered a bit, "because for some people they use their left hand for other things."

"Like what?" They were not going to give up the pursuit of understanding why we use the right hand versus the left.

"You see," I started in, fumbling already, "in some parts of the world, they use their left hand when they go to the potty, so the right hand is cleaner."

"What? Cleaning poop?" They giggled, smirked, then burst out laughing, each in rapid succession. We had clearly already lost our focus here. (Leave it to bathroom activity of any sort to derail children from concentrating on the task at hand.)

"Okay, okay, let's pay attention here." I tried to regain order. "Another reason we use our right hand is to show we come in peace, without a weapon in our hand."

"Couldn't we have a weapon in our left hand?" Jack asked.

Sigh. "I suppose so." I needed a different approach.

"We will use our right hand because I say so!" That made sense to them. They quieted down, and I continued with the demonstration.

"All right now, as is our custom, open your right hand, palm up, turned a little on its side, facing the other person. Grasp their hand and give it a good, firm shake, up and down, very briefly. Now, look into each other's eyes, smile, and introduce yourself as if meeting for the first time. This will definitely give a good first impression of friendliness and confidence."

Learning the skill of the proper handshake is still a work in progress, but here's an upshot worth mentioning. About a year later, a good friend of mine who owns her own law firm met Jack for the first time. Shortly after she left I received a text from her saying, "I am impressed with Jack! He looked me directly in the eye and gave me a firm, confident handshake. At thirteen years old, he has a wonderful presence."

Was I smiling from ear to ear? You bet I was.

ACTIVITY: HANDSHAKES

In today's world of tweets and digital interactions, handshakes are becoming a lost art. Too bad. I think we grandparents can do something about that. We can reintroduce the skill that involves eye contact, goodwill, and straightforward human connection. Handshakes are the first step in building a good relationship. Reaching out to another—this is something you can easily do with your grandchildren.

What Kids Will Learn

- The value of personal touch
- How to demonstrate respect
- The nature of a first impression
- How to create trust in a matter of seconds
- The value of eye contact in creating a stronger human connection

What You Need

Nothing but good intentions and practice. And of course, face-to-face time with one or more grandchildren.

What You'll Do

Shake hands! Just in case you need a refresher, here are the basics:

1. Face the person you are greeting.

2. Extend your right hand.

3. Open your hand; turn it a little on its side.

4. Grasp the other person's open hand and give it a firm shake, up and down.

5. Look into the other person's eyes, smile, and introduce yourself or say hello.

Once they get the hang of it, you can suggest they offer a handshake when they meet their new teacher, coach, or parent of a friend.

Time Required

Not much. Probably fifteen minutes will do it.

Tips

- Practice whenever you are together. Then you can hug.
- This is an activity best suited for children ages five and older.

Adding value through outings and adventures

CHAPTER EIGHT:

UNDERSTANDING WHAT YOU HAVE TO OFFER

Clearly, as our handshaking episode proved, life is messy, and when there is no order to be made of the chaos, only your sense of humor will get you through. Some mix of self-reliance and teamwork factors into everything you strive to do in life, and it helps to understand people. But first you must understand yourself, and nothing helps you get to know yourself better than a challenge.

As I mentioned before, I started my adult career late and in sales. I learned a lot about myself by selling on commission. Though I grant you it is not for everyone, I found it empowering. I started out earning a salary and bonus (based on sales), selling advertising for the Yellow Pages and eventually jumped to straight commission at a commercial real estate company. Straight commission means you earn a percentage of sales volume but with no salary, no safety net. You are paid solely on your performance, that's it. There were no set hours to my days, no manager directing what I did with my time. Straight commission means it's entirely up to you to produce, and you have to figure out how to do it (while differentiating yourself from the competition—that value-added stuff).

That can be scary when you're a single parent. It was for me. Those first weeks I wanted to crawl under my desk and hide. *I can't do this! I don't know where to start! How will I pay my bills and feed my family?* I knew I had two choices: sink or swim. I chose to swim, hard and fast. I kept reminding myself of what I knew about myself. I did a lot of self-talk with encouragement. "It's okay, Marianne," I'd tell myself. "You know how to sell. You like to work with people and you care about them, and you like to be helpful and solve problems. You can do this." And I did.

I started talking with people in the business. I learned all over again the power of relationships. By their experience and advice, I slowly developed my own network, my own support team, and my own client base. And I found ways to add value. I wasn't afraid to be myself even if it meant doing the unexpected.

One time in particular I was brokering a real estate negotiation that wasn't going well. I was representing a major grocery store that wanted to build on a vacant ten-acre parcel. We met with the property owner several times, but he didn't want to sell. They couldn't come to terms that were mutually agreeable. I knew that to get them talking again would be difficult, but I asked for the meeting anyway and they agreed. The conversation again took a negative turn, and my client got up to leave. Something had to be done. I reached into my briefcase and brought out a bag of homemade chocolate chip cookies I had baked the night before (anticipating I might need a backup plan).

I put the cookies on the table. The two men looked at me, then looked at each other. Neither one said a word. I poured coffee, passed the cookies, and suggested we discuss where they might find common ground. The upshot? They reached an agreement with a fair price and terms. The supermarket opened in the new location (and has been doing business there for over twenty years as of the writing of this book). A win-win for all.

Though cookies may not work in all situations, I can assure you cookie-cutter solutions don't either. You have to learn to trust your instincts. I've learned it's okay to be yourself, to put aside the fear of being different, and to do the unexpected. In school, I was both a cheerleader *and* the class president. (I've never been too keen on stereotypes.)

Now I think back on all those past learning experiences and realize that it's all been leading me to this moment. I am able to see my grandchildren for who they are, as individuals, and to adapt to their different styles and personalities. I can respect their differences and possibly reach them on a personal level that others, like teachers and friends, can't or don't try. I can apply my accumulation of knowledge to the next generation to help them navigate the world. From every struggle I've had, to every accomplishment I've earned, there had to be a nugget or two of human experience I could transfer to my grandchildren.

And this is what every grandparent does or can do to some degree. I think most grandparents don't realize what a value they are to the kids. They do so much more for the family than saving a few bucks in babysitting costs. I'm not one who can shut down my professional side. The corporate executive is alive and well, albeit working in a different environment. And the kid in me is here, too, down deep, and now reawakened with my grandchildren. Spending time with them has brought me full circle. I bring to each experience the child, the young mother, the career woman, the wife, the friend. It all adds up. I'm all in all over again. I'm showing them how to be a grown-up, and they are showing me how to be a kid again. Every healthy relationship is an exchange, and this flow keeps the Camp Grandma initiative balanced and evolving.

ACTIVITY: SHARE MORE OF YOURSELF WITH YOUR GRANDCHILDREN

Grandparents have much to offer grandchildren, which makes the role of the grandparent one of tremendous opportunity and potential. If you're determined to build strong and lasting relationships with your grandchildren, then share more of yourself with them. Let them know who you are as an individual, not just as the parent of one of their parents. It will help enrich their lives and develop emotional bonds that will last a lifetime.

What Kids Will Learn

- How to learn and grow from life experiences
- Family history
- New skills
- The importance of family
- How to overcome adversity
- That older people can be cool

What You Need

Commitment to the goal of sharing more of yourself and quality *time* together with your grandchildren. A notepad may be helpful to capture ideas and thoughts that come to mind.

What You'll Do

1. Start by doing a self-assessment of your life. Hold up the mirror. Who do you see? Look past the lines and graying hair to the person within. How would you describe yourself? By your accomplishments? Skills you learned along the way? Your values, your experiences, your relationships, your career? Make a list of what you consider important.

2. Ask yourself what you learned from life. Maybe it's just the simplest thing like learning right from wrong. Consider what you like about your life. Consider your challenges. This is just to get you thinking of what you have to offer. It's not so much what you did, it's what you learned from life that is there within you to share with your grandchildren. List what lessons you learned.

3. Decide how you can teach those lessons. Think of stories you can tell. Find old pictures that show an experience or time in your life that was meaningful. Share an interest or an activity you like and explain why it is important to you.

Time Required

As long as it takes to connect in meaningful and impactful ways.

Tips

- Start now—it's never too early or too late to let you shine!
- Don't worry if you live some distance away or are not in frequent contact with your grandchildren. Anytime you connect can be meaningful if you are open and giving of yourself to the process.

Learning about other cultures

CHAPTER NINE:

TEAMWORK

I t occurred to me that one of the best ways to learn about yourself is through interaction with others. So introducing the concept of teams along with the power and value of teamwork made perfect sense for Camp Grandma.

In my working years I'd observed that, by combining strengths and skills with a clear objective, a team could build efficiencies and consistently achieve better results than a group of individuals operating separately. It's the two-heads-are-better-than-one scenario.

The key to a successful team is matching or identifying complementary skills to balance strengths with weaknesses or shortcomings. It doesn't work to just throw a group of people together and expect a positive outcome. Matching people with different strengths and letting them utilize those strengths brings out the best in all while filling the gaps where a weakness might exist. A functioning team can be a powerful force, an illuminating experience. It takes the strength to trust yourself and others and requires self-knowledge. Understanding one's strengths and weaknesses is a common business practice, one that accepts the fact that none of us can do (or like to do) everything well. In the real estate business, it was easy to identify those who were the business generators and those who preferred to manage transactions. Some were go-getters, while others favored a steadier, more deliberate pace. Everyone brought their own uniqueness to the organization, and all skills and characteristics were important. Knowing who was who was valuable because then you could team up with others with complementary skills to do what each liked or were best at doing, while providing the best service to your clients.

So, what comes easily to you? What do you like doing? These are probably your strengths. Conversely, what you find difficult and what you put off doing are most likely weaknesses. Learning to focus on your strengths and manage your weaknesses leads to a more productive life in general, since your strengths are great indicators of how you will be successful. Understanding your strengths and allowing the grandkids' strengths also to lead you in making choices will be your guide in developing your own style as a mentor-grandparent.

At Camp Grandma, though, I'm not working with folks who have established skill sets that I can identify and match up. I'm working with children who are growing and changing all the time. They are developing their own interests and learning where their strengths might lie. In effect they were thrown together at Camp Grandma, yes, but that wasn't going to stop me from setting up some teamwork activities.

I LOVE MAPS

"Who wants to go on a treasure hunt?" I asked one afternoon, as Camp Grandma was beginning to take shape, when Lauren was five, Katie was seven, Jake was eight, and Jack was ten years old.

"We do, we do!" the girls gleefully exclaimed.

"What treasure?" Jack asked suspiciously.

Jake closed his book and walked over to understand more about what I had just suggested.

To backtrack just a moment, I should tell you I love maps. True, though printed maps may not be as popular or necessary as they once were, I still think knowing how to read one may come in handy. Who knows, one day your GPS may decide not to function (mine is temperamental as it is). Technology hasn't dampened my interest in maps. With satellite imagery and the shrinking and expanding screens, I can zoom in and out and am fascinated by the depth of layered information available at my fingertips. Not only do maps tell me how to get where I'm going, they give me a sense of place. Maps tell stories of the world around us with perspective. So the concept of a treasure hunt made perfect sense to me. I thought, *Not only will I introduce my grandchildren to map reading, but we will see how readily they work together to find the treasure.*

Our treasure hunt went like this:

To prepare, I put inexpensive colored "gems" in small net bags and hid them all around the backyard. Then I made maps directing the grandkids to clues for finding these treasures. I made two sets of maps, one more challenging for the two older boys and a simpler one with more pictures for the two younger girls.

I divided them into two teams (to practice their collaboration and communication skills). They were excited to begin. I handed out the maps.

Lauren, the most excited about this activity, took one look at the map and cried out in distress, "Grandma, I can't read yet!"

"I can," Katie chimed in. "Why don't I read the directions, and you can be the one to pick up the treasures we find?"

Lauren happily nodded in agreement. Problem solved. Teamwork begun. Out the door they went.

When the boys got their map, I heard Jack suggest, "Why don't we take turns reading the clues?"

Jake responded with an affirmative nod while flying out the door to see what treasures he could spot without the help of clues on the map.

Jack ran after him and started reading, "Go to lemon tree, turn left and go up five stairs, turn right at the balcony and—hey, I found it. Your turn, Jake."

The boys were first to collect all the treasures. Jake approached the activity with his typical focus and determination as if to say, *Treasures found, mission accomplished.* Jack, more methodical, followed the directions step-by-step, hoping I think for a pot of gold or something of real value to be uncovered at the end of his quest. As you might have guessed, the boys weren't exactly thrilled with their treasures. *What are we going to do with gaudy colored glass in net bags?* they might have been wondering.

But the girls were delighted with all the sparkly gems. "Oh, look! A purple diamond!"

Fortunately for the boys, I have a small treasure chest with inexpensive toys that I keep on hand if they earn a reward. For being good team players and finding all their treasure, they each picked a prize from the chest that day, and they all went home happy.

A few years and countless treasure hunts later, Katie's dad was telling me about a trip the family took to the La Brea Tar Pits in Los Angeles. "I was really surprised and impressed," he said. "Katie was using the map/guide and directed us all around the attraction."

Ha! It was no surprise to me.

PERFORMING

Another great team-building exercise for the four of them is when they put on a performance.

One afternoon, Katie picked up a red wool scarf of mine and announced, "Let's all do a play about Little Red Riding Hood, and I'll be her."

"What part will I play?" Lauren asked, then went about solving the problem. Noticing my blue shawl, she suggested a story about two sisters going to visit their grandma. "We can call it Red Riding Hood and her sister Blue!" she exclaimed.

"I'll be the wolf," said Jake, as he ran off in search of a wolf costume.

Jack emphatically declared, "I am not going to play the grandmother, so I won't be in the play."

"But Jack, you have to be in the play," Katie and Lauren pleaded. "We need you."

"No way, it's okay, I'll just watch." But as he watched the others practice their parts, he observed nothing but chaos and confusion.

"Let's skip together to Grandmother's house. Okay, this way. No! She lives in the woods, the woods are that way!"

"Jake, not yet! It's not time to bite the grandmother! We will tell you when . . . stay out of sight. Don't growl yet, it's not time!"

Clearly they needed a director. But instead of taking part behind-the-scenes, Jack announced, "I'll be the narrator!" With this role, he took it upon himself to establish some order.

"Grandma, what does a narrator wear?" he asked.

"Let's see. Maybe a jacket and tie."

Jake was also perplexed over what his wolf would wear. So together we went searching in my closet and settled on a black sequined jacket and tie for the narrator and a black coat, black hat, and black mask for the wolf.

Well, the play was a success. What I liked about it was that they collaboratively modified the story to fit their individual skill sets and interests, and they did so mostly on the fly, which is how teamwork succeeds in the corporate world as well.

They were the actors and also assumed the roles of scriptwriter, director, and even producer (when they went looking for costumes and props). They did their share of problem solving since right from the start they uncovered conflicts (in choosing roles and costumes), much like life, and much like what it takes to be productive in the world. Working together toward a common goal, they demonstrated their ability to compromise and cooperate and care about each other's needs, not just their own.

COOKIES, ANYONE?

Another activity we turn into a team-building exercise is cooking. We all like to eat, so cooking is a natural with kids. Let me rephrase that. We all like sweets, so baking cookies with your grandchildren is a popular activity for all grandmothers. At Camp Grandma I like to introduce them to favorite family recipes that we can make together. This way they are learning a bit about family as well as working as a team to accomplish a task. It might be my daughter's childhood favorite, tapioca pudding, or my son's favorite, grasshopper pie, or Grandma's sugar or super chocolate chip cookies, but we choose something to make together.

"Grandma, can we make cookies today?"

"Sure, we have time," I replied.

Lauren rushed to get the stool.

Katie asked, "Can I crack the eggs?"

"I want to crack the eggs, too, Grandma," said Lauren.

"Okay, look at the recipe, girls. How many eggs do we need?"

"We need two," Katie exclaimed. "I'll do one and Lauren can do one."

Jack said, "I'll run the mixer. Jake, do you want to help?" "No, thank you." He was more interested in building a solar system out of Play-Doh.

I like that they are exposed to the basics of cooking, which includes reading recipes, math (fractions) when measuring, how to safely use knives and appliances, clean up, and so on. So far, we have primarily made sweets, but surely we will soon start to expand with other food groups.

I thought it could be fun to collect family recipes for a book, based on individual favorites and sharing a little history with each entry. This is clearly an ongoing project and one I think many grandmothers do for their families. Doing it will take some time, but I bet I know where I can get some help.

THE BIG PICTURE

Clearly, I am in the thick of all these activities and team projects at Camp Grandma, making maps for treasure hunts, playing ol' granny in an impromptu play, or orchestrating a cooking adventure. But I observe as I go along. I observe them shaping their roles when together, demonstrating strengths that come naturally. Jack responsibly takes the lead as the oldest. He's the ringleader they look up to, to assure them things are always done right. Lauren, though the youngest, motivates and organizes them all with her creative ideas and amazing social and problem-solving skills. Katie is always a dependable team player, cooperative, willing to contribute, meticulous with detail, and creative with her designs.

Jake is our expert on space, art, and origami, among other curious things. Though he enjoys being part of the group, he is never afraid to demonstrate his independence and freethinking in pursuit of more intellectual activities. He is free to do so, and I often wonder, *Is he feeling the loose but strong tether between us even when he is not in the room with us?* I sense so. I hope so. Perhaps he is the explorer among us of a frontier we will all cross into someday, when childhood experiences like Camp Grandma are no longer locked into a specific time and place but rather a reservoir of all that has flowed between us and always will.

I like to think that all the kids are learning they are free to be their own person. If it happens that they are not immediately within the physical vicinity of the main team activity, that doesn't mean they are not part of the team. There are many ways to engage and different levels of engagement, some felt though unseen. In the business world you feel the support of a good manager and that fuels your taking initiative to solve problems on your own even when he or she is not around. In a family with working parents, a child may miss their company when apart. But the child's awareness that their work is for the benefit of the family means the child may not feel the distance between them in their hearts. (So maybe the child pitches in and does the dishes without being asked once in a while.) It's all part of what we call a team and the connection that comes from belonging.

As my grandchildren are getting older and more active with school, scouts, sports, and other interests, it is harder to get them all together as often as I did. So sometimes it's just three or maybe two of them. Sometimes it's just one plus Grandma. That's okay. It is what it is. We still have fun collaborating together in experiencing new adventures and learning new things. We bring our own gifts to the effort and cooperate to achieve the end result.

ACTIVITY: TEAM BUILDING

To foster the notion of *teamwork,* set a goal or create a project your grandchildren can work on with you and each other. You'll have fun together working cooperatively toward a shared purpose.

What Kids Will Learn

- How to work with others
- How to move from thinking only of themselves to consideration of others
- How to strengthen social and emotional skills
- How to be accountable
- How to build self-confidence

What You Need

An idea for a team-based activity your grandchildren will like. Draw from your interests as well but consider ball games, craft projects, games, plays, baking, gardening, and chores. Yes, doing chores together like washing a car or doing laundry can turn into fun team activities too.

Collect the necessary materials. For instance, to bake a cake for Mom's birthday, you'll need a recipe, a shopping list of ingredients, time to do shopping, and of course baking supplies. If you choose making a Christmas gift for

Dad, you can brainstorm with your grandchildren for ideas and then collect what is needed together—that can be the first team-bonding activity. If you want to plant a vegetable garden, you'll need a layout based on space available, plants and tools for gardening, and so on.

What You'll Do

1. Start by outlining the objective with your grandchildren.

2. Talk about tasks needed to complete the project.

3. Assign tasks based on the skills of team members (you can always draw in more people if necessary).

4. Discuss the importance of everyone's participation and commitment to the goal.

For example, let's go back to the cake for Mom: "Would you like to help me bake a cake for Mom's birthday? We'll need to do the shopping for the ingredients, bake it, frost and decorate it, then present it to Mom, singing 'Happy Birthday.' What parts would you like to do (aside from eating it, of course)?"

And go on from there.

Whatever you decide to do together will be important. It really doesn't matter what you choose. It's the *together* part and the working side by side for a common purpose that creates value and will enrich their lives, and yours.

Time Required

This will vary depending on the activity, number of children involved, and their ages. It could take as little as an hour if you decide to, say, wash the car together (or an afternoon to dry their clothes after they squirted each other with the hose). It could take several hours if you decide to put on a play or go on a treasure hunt. It could last months if you decide to grow a vegetable garden, with regular increments of fifteen minutes to go outside and look at it, fifteen minutes to pull weeds, or thirty minutes to pick berries.

Tips

- Teamwork works best once the child is at least five years old. Before that, you can certainly do things together, but the concept of assigning tasks to accomplish an objective may be too hard to grasp for a younger child.
- Watch for characteristics in your grandchildren that could translate into activities with others. For instance, do you notice a competitive streak? Then start a competition like "Who can grow the biggest cauliflower?" Or in an older child, do you recognize teaching tendencies that could be useful when doing a craft with a range of ages, giving them a leadership role? Or let the younger child draw the face on the Halloween pumpkin and the older one use the knife to hollow it out.

- Don't expect that cake to turn out as you might have expected. Drowned in sprinkles, it just might become your new favorite. And who cares if the clothes aren't folded perfectly? Once they are on your body, you won't notice a crease or two.

Sculpting with shaving cream

CHAPTER TEN:

BUILDING YOUR RÉSUMÉ

Afterteaching my grandkids so many other life skills, I
decided it was time to help them write their résumés.
It was my intention that we would update them periodically, at least once a year. You might be asking, "How
in the world can that happen? Kids haven't lived that long,
how can they write a résumé?" Well, they can, and it's only
a little tricky.

PLAN AHEAD

A résumé helps you acquire the *job* you want. Right? How
about starting in your youth and writing a résumé for the
life you want? We typically write résumés looking back-
ward: Where did we go to college? What jobs did we have?
How many years here or there?

At Camp Grandma, we reversed the direction. We looked back so we could plan ahead. I wanted my grandchildren to experience the process of reflecting on what they'd done so far, at whatever age, so that they might make better decisions about what they do going forward. I wanted to teach them to consider long-term results and the effects and consequences of their choices and behavior, starting now. So I asked, "What do you want on your résumé?"

This idea came to me one day when the kids were writing in their journals about experiences they'd had at Camp Grandma. They were writing about *what* they did and *when* they did it. It reminded me of writing résumés, one of the most common tasks in the working world. It occurred to me that if they started early in life to account for their choices and accomplishments, it might get them thinking about future decisions they make.

I wanted to keep this exercise simple, so I brushed off my notes on writing a résumé, something I'd used several times in my career when coaching or for my personal use, and chose the four most important topics to address.

"Hey everyone, let's sit around the table. I have a new exercise you might like."

"What exercise?" They cautiously approached the table. As with everything pertaining to Camp Grandma, they were curious but a bit wary about what in the heck I'd come up with next.

"We're going to learn to write résumés. A résumé is a document that includes education, experience, skills, and accomplishments used to apply for jobs."

"What? Are you making us get a job?" Katie's eyes were wide with fear.

"I'm too young to go to work, Grandma. Please don't make me," Lauren pleaded.

"I'm not making you go to work now. We're just practicing so you will know what to do when you are older and want to get a job. Let me show you." And I handed each a list with four categories:

1. Education . . . . School you attend or have attended

2. Experience . . . . Travel, lessons, volunteer activities

3. Accomplishments . . Awards, recognition, or some sense of personal satisfaction

4. Strengths . . . . What are you good at doing?

They looked puzzled. "What are we supposed to do with this?" They were understandably skeptical. I'd grown used to the look.

"I want you to tell me about yourself, what you have done or learned so far in life, in these four categories. For example, under education, put what grade you are in and what school you are attending."

"Oh, that's easy," they all said in unison with a sigh of relief and quickly began writing.

We continued with each topic with a fair amount of coaching on my part, as you might imagine. They came up with the answers themselves, though, and I loved them.

When asked about strengths, Jack said he was "responsible" (no surprise there), and Lauren asserted that her strength was that she is "very, very nice." So true.

Under the topic of accomplishments, they all said they didn't have any. So I asked, "What about recognition as Student of the Month, or a Citizenship Award, or for participation in a sporting or musical event?" I already knew the answers. Once they started thinking about it, they were calling out one achievement after another, and their lists grew. They were beginning to realize all they had accomplished in their young lives.

After they finished with their writing, we talked about what they wrote. We discussed how their education, strengths, accomplishments, and experiences might help them when they were grown-up.

"Jack, how will being responsible help you get a job?"

"Well, I think it will help others know I can get stuff done and I won't make excuses."

"Jake, you list reading books as an accomplishment. Why is that important?"

"Because books help me grow."

"What can you learn from taking surfing lessons, Jake?"

"To surf," he answered.

Well, I asked. And I intend to keep asking because I've planted the seed and introduced the concept of self-analysis. Asking yourself and answering yourself is a process that factors into a healthy life. At the very least, just my asking and being interested demonstrates my support. They matter to me, and so what they do matters as well.

AN ONGOING PROCESS

Though the actual résumé revamping is only an annual activity, it's my hope that their awareness of building a résumé continues throughout the year. Periodically I will ask them, "What do you think you might like to do when you are grown-up?" "Who might you like to be?" "What do you think you might need to get you there?" I realize they might not have any of these answers now, and even if they do, those answers will change again and again, but asking keeps them thinking. And thinking is part of preparation and training for achievement. Training their minds to visualize what they want out of life and of themselves could enable them to make choices today that are more aligned with the person they'd like to be. So, too, can all of us, of course; just as it's never too early, it's never too late to change, to set your sights higher.

By actually planning their résumés, kids begin goal setting. They start considering how their activities and friends define them. I encourage my grandkids to think about how they spend their time. For example: What do they gain from the time they spend practicing their music? Going to swimming lessons? Playing with friends? Watching TV? How are these activities important to them? Or will they be, later in life?

I recently heard from a friend whose teenage son was bound for college. She was surprised that some colleges are now actually requesting a résumé if you want a scholarship or internship position. Well, at Camp Grandma we are getting a head start on that process.

Under the experience category, all the kids listed travel. I think this is wonderful. Their parents have done a great job of taking them on lots of outings and vacations, and it is clearly recognized as a value to the grandchildren. Popular culture is right in identifying the passport as the "new diploma." I couldn't agree more. Travel is a terrific learning tool, and while the cost may be prohibitive for many families, the mind is not limited. With magazines, the local library, and the Internet, the mind can access books, stories, and images that transport the imagination to faraway places. You can experience the joy and wonder of exploration and discovery for free. Good writing evokes sounds and smells, the sensory links that embed the travel experience into vivid memory.

We recently had a "faraway" experience, which is travel without getting on a plane, to add to our résumés. Near my home there is a Hindu temple authentically constructed out of marble and Indian pink sandstone. This is a traditional Indian mandir with spires seventy-eight feet tall. The intricate carvings and colorful decorations are reminiscent of one that actually exists in New Delhi. One day we picked up stakes and had a Camp Grandma adventure to India via our local temple.

"Hey, Grandma, why do we have to take off our shoes?" Katie asked.

"It's a sign of respect."

"I bet the floor stays cleaner too," Lauren piped in.

"Yup, I bet it does." And I smiled.

We had a great time, learning a little about the Hindu faith and how the temple was constructed. We experienced a bit of India and even tasted India when we sampled cookies made from an authentic Indian recipe. Jake later told me his favorite Camp Grandma memory was visiting the temple with his cousins.

Writing our résumés continues to be, as it was intended, a work in progress just like training and preparation, based on the idea that how you spend your time is important and what you do now can benefit you later in life. Hopefully by introducing this concept at an early age, it will help them consider what they have to offer the world in applying themselves to reach their full potential. I will continue to collect their responses to keep for them as reference. It will be exciting and interesting to see how they build their résumés as the years go by. We have only just begun.

If we could do it all over again, how might we have answered, "What do you want on your résumé?"

ACTIVITY: BUILDING A RÉSUMÉ

By introducing the concept of writing résumés early in life, your grandchildren get a glimpse of what they will be asked to do as an adult. Résumés provide a summary of your experiences, skills, and accomplishments. Traditionally they are a primary tool in a job search, but for kids they are a tool to help them mindfully recognize how they've spent their time and hopefully make good choices on what they do going forward. A résumé may be requested for college and scholarship applications, as well as prospective employment.

What Kids Will Learn

- How to think and reflect on the past as it relates to the present and future
- How to look at themselves from another's point of view
- To be aware of the connection between action and consequences
- How to visualize what they want
- How to set goals
- How to market themselves

What You Need

A notebook for each grandchild is recommended. A paper and pencil will do, but a notebook is something you can add to as the years go by. And it's another great keepsake for them for reflection and review.

What You'll Do

1. On the first page of the notebook, enter the child's name and age with the date, then write down these topics:

- Education
- Experience
- Accomplishments
- Strengths

2. Sit down with your grandchildren and ask them to write down something about themselves under these first three headings: the number of years of schooling they have had; the experiences they remember that were meaningful;

awards, participation in scouting, church choir, musical recitals, and so on.

3. Then ask them what they think are their strengths—what they are good at doing.

4. Once they are finished, talk about what they have done and how it might help them when they are grown-up.

5. Review these annually with your grandchildren and watch them build their résumés as the years go by.

Time Required

Depending on how much conversation results from the experience, this should take about an hour.

Tips

- Buy a notebook for yourself so you can make notes to capture the comments and remarks of your grandchildren as they are completing this exercise.
- Encourage them to determine which of their activities have little to no value. Hopefully they will learn to see this for themselves and make more appropriate choices, focusing on a more productive use of their time. (Fingers crossed.)

"Faraway" experience to Hindu temple

CHAPTER ELEVEN:

RELATIONSHIPS

"Why the long face? What's the matter?" I asked Lauren, who was sitting on the couch quietly with sad eyes.

"Katie doesn't want to be my friend anymore." She rested her face on her hands and sighed.

"That would surprise me." I put my arm around her for comfort. "Just give her a little time to herself. Sometimes we all need a little alone time."

Just then, Katie entered the room. "Hi, Lauren. Do you want to do a pony story?"

Lauren jumped up with a wide smile. They hugged and off they went. The world was a happy place again.

BUILDING RELATIONSHIPS

What is better than a great relationship, be it with a parent, a child, a spouse, a sibling, a friend, a coworker? Nothing. No career, money, or possessions can equal a true friend. And where is there a better place to grow these relationships than within family? Webster's Dictionary defines "family" as "a group of people who are related to each other," which to me means that family can be limitless: related by birth or choice; natural, adopted, or extended. No matter the size, family implies that the people within the group are in some way important to each other or they wouldn't call each other family.

Camp Grandma, when all is said and done, is about bringing my family—in particular, my grandchildren—together to build deep and lasting relationships. We are by nature social beings, but children are not typically born with the ability to form good relationships. Their early years tend to be self-focused, and learning the skills necessary to build friendships takes time and patience. We all enjoy being understood and accepted for who we are, but this only happens over time. Camp Grandma provides this time to really get to know one another in a safe and trusting environment, over years of being in each other's company.

At Camp Grandma, building relationships is a priority, not only for me with each of the kids but also with each other as siblings and cousins. With time together they learn to trust and respect one another, as well as to know what is important to each other, which includes their likes and dislikes.

For cousins Lauren and Katie, friendship came easily. They are close in age and share similar interests. They like the same toys: Legos, My Little Pony, Shopkins, and other tiny cute playthings. Neither is particularly interested in dolls. They love going to plays and musical events and can play for hours with stories they make up with their toys, even going so far as to draw up playbills or little books to accompany the story line. Though very different in personality, they complement one another in behavior and sincerely care for each other.

Observing my granddaughters, Lauren is definitely more high energy and socially driven. She is also more physically active. Katie is quieter by nature, tends to be more focused, and is less inclined to change activities as often. She knows she requires downtime to recharge her batteries when she tires of an activity and is learning how to ask for it. Lauren is learning that this is not a reflection on her when Katie needs her quiet time.

I like to give them their space to work out any differences. Small arguments between kids can be good learning experiences. Way back when I was growing up, we never had supervised playdates. We'd go out in the neighborhood and find friends. I remember well those formative years with several friends who lived near my home. We'd ride bikes, put on performances, do all sorts of things together, and, yes, get into tiffs on occasion. It was not unusual for me to leave in a huff, storm into my house, slam the door, and vow to never play with my friend ever again. Then the phone would ring.

"Do you want to come over?"

"Sure, I'll be right there."

I know these experiences were valuable. With no one overseeing our behavior, we learned to work it out for ourselves. We learned to forgive and to say we're sorry. Maybe most importantly, we learned to give and take when resolving our differences. You might say this was an early experience in conflict resolution, a way to find peaceful solutions, which I know has helped me better deal with people throughout my life.

When I was working and managing a real estate office, I was frequently asked to settle commission disputes. Two brokers would walk into my office, usually under duress, and want me to settle their misunderstanding, each hoping I would take a side in their favor. After hearing them out, typically I'd ask them to leave my office and work it out between themselves. I always added, "If you can't do this, then come back in and I'll settle it, but I can guarantee neither of you will like my decision," implying that they wouldn't get all they wanted. That got their attention, and we rarely had to address the situation again. It's amazing what we all can do when we know it is up to us to work things out. All it takes is effort and believing you can.

Jack and Jake, on the other hand, are completely different boys without much in common. You would not find them playing together on the playground if they both attended the same school, unlike Katie and Lauren who might find each other because of common interests. Jack is two years older and more social, although he's more likely to be head down in a video game these days. Jake loves school and is curious about and interested in many varied topics. Yet they have come to appreciate each other and their differences. Jake says Jack is the best video game player and likes Jack's songs and goofiness. Jack is quick to compliment Jake on any number of his abilities, from boogie boarding to origami designs.

I like that there is no negative competition between them. When they are together there is a sense of comfort, even as they share the same space without saying a word. They accept each other for who they are and are content in each other's company. I sense a feeling of respect for one another, a critical component of friendship.

Jack validated this for me recently. We were casually talking together, and he started telling me how he felt about his cousin Jake. "Jake and I have a lot more in common than most people think," he said. "In a way I am a lot like him. We've been through many of the same things. I feel connected to him, not just as family. He's grown a lot, and so have I. He has qualities I wish I had. He's unaffected by the world's influences. If a kid calls him a name, he doesn't react, he just goes along his way. He is a kind soul, wouldn't hurt anybody. If anyone I know is going to heaven, it's Jake."

What Jack expressed was not only complimentary of his cousin but showed incredible insight for a fourteen-year-old. Jack had learned to see past their differences and had come to recognize Jake's strengths and to appreciate the ways they are alike. Would they have come to this understanding had it not been for Camp Grandma? Maybe. But here they have been able to find common ground, so to speak, sharing in some activities they both like while accepting and respecting their differences. Jack likes to draw and is quite good at it. Jake loves art and likes to see what Jack designs. Both love Legos and are able to build intricate and elaborate pieces. They also build with clay and sculpture with shaving cream (a favorite).

LIFETIME CONNECTIONS

I believe that all four of my grandkids will be there for each other as the years go by. While they know it's important to me, I believe they'll grow to appreciate having each other as a resource and maybe even a lifeline. The time at Camp Grandma is already helping develop an identity they all share. They have memories of singing and dancing together, playing games and learning new things, being active and going on outings. Whatever the circumstance, they were in it together.

Since Jack is the oldest, I recently asked him what his fondest memories are of Camp Grandma.

"Mostly you, Grandma. The T-shirts you had made for us. I think of the picture you have of all of us. It's all good. I think of the social interaction, family, new ways of seeing things around you. It's like school, but not school. I remember the new experiences."

I trust they will draw off this history (as well as the times to come) to assist them with new relationships and experiences. They are learning to trust, respect, openly communicate, and appreciate each other both for ways they are alike and for differences as well. What I hope they take away from this is that for lasting friendships, you must be willing to invest time and energy. It will also require compromise and commitment. Building true lasting relationships is not easy, but anything worthwhile seldom is. The good news is that doing it well can last a lifetime.

When I asked the kids why family is important, their responses were varied:

Katie said, "Because they take care of you and get you out of pickles."

Lauren said, "To have loving people in your life."

Jack said, "They tolerate your crap."

Jake said, "Because they get along with each other."

As for my relationships with them? Each is unique and special, as each child is unique and special. I spend more time with some but miss more time with others. I love how one is so much like me, but I love every bit as much that the others are unlike me. Some are more responsive, others harder to get to know, but I love the challenge. With my grandchildren, I am in the best company. I mean, come on, how bad can the world be if it has your grandchildren in it, right?

ACTIVITY: DEVELOPING RELATIONSHIPS

Understanding the value of relationships at an early age is a tremendous advantage. We aren't born knowing how to build great relationships, so the skill to do so has to be learned. By knowing how to develop healthy and positive relationships with others, your grandchildren will have a head start to a life that feels more satisfied, supported, and connected.

What Kids Will Learn

- How to get along with others
- How to behave and communicate
- How to value companionship
- How to feel cared for and supported
- How to trust others
- How to need others
- How to accept differences in others
- How to love and be loved

What You Need

To make the commitment. Be willing to invest in the relationship with your time and attention. Any meaningful relationship takes energy and effort. Ask yourself, *What kind of relationship do I want with my grandchildren?* Be mindful of your true intentions and then go about making it happen. Be proactive, not reactive. Set a goal to connect every day, week, or month. Build this commitment into your schedule and enjoy the rewards.

Be present with them. From near or far, engage. Be with them in the moment. If you can't be with them in person, then call or text or write a note or letter. If you live some distance apart, you might send a video of you reading a bedtime story or telling a story about yourself at their age. There's an app called Story Bug, which gives grandparents and grandchildren the opportunity to read together. However you are able, just connect!

What You'll Do

1. Take an interest by getting to know them. In order to build a meaningful and positive relationship you must understand them—know their likes, dislikes, and habits. Ask questions—lots of questions—and then listen, really listen to what they have to say. Take what they say seriously and respond accordingly. Get to know "their story" as you share yours. This validates their individuality, builds understanding, and shows you care.

2. Be real, and don't be afraid to show your vulnerability. Showing vulnerability is what separates a relationship from an acquaintance. You can keep it at a treetop level or go deeper to build a lifetime bond. This goes hand in hand with being honest and telling them the truth, which builds trust. And by watching you deal with difficulty, they learn by your example how to deal with adversity and develop their own resiliency.

3. Respect them. Most of us were told to respect our elders. But what better way to teach your grandchildren how to respect others than to show them how it feels to be respected? Recognize them as their own person, no matter how big or small. We are all individuals, and the sooner they feel valued for their uniqueness and appreciated for who they are, the better they will be for it.

4. Create memories. Share in activities and common interests or teach them something new (or let them teach you something new). From baking cookies to travel experiences, from fishing to watching their ball game, it really doesn't matter, as long as you are connecting and experiencing the comfort and joy of being together.

5. Be a cheerleader by acknowledging, complimenting, and praising them when deserved. Look for ways to bolster their self-esteem so they feel seen and their efforts are recognized. Be positive and constructive in your comments, which might help them view the world more optimistically.

Time Required

Any or as much as you have to give. It's the quality of your time together that will count the most.

Tips

- Don't expect young children to run up to you with a hug just because you have the title of grandparent. As with any meaningful relationship, their affection and respect must be earned. As the grown-up, it's up to you to do the work. Your relationship might feel one-sided at first, but in time, your feelings will be reciprocated.
- Don't feel as a grandparent that to be loved you have to be lax and indulgent. Being firm when appropriate actually shows you care and want what is best for them. Set boundaries and show by example how saying no might be for their own good.

- Developing a relationship with your grandchildren and caring for their needs might actually
extend your life! I've read that grandparents who
are active in the care of their grandchildren live
longer than those that don't by up to five years.
As if we needed another reason to be close.

Jack and Jake

Lauren and Katie

CHAPTER TWELVE:

PLAN YOUR WORK AND WORK YOUR PLAN

O ne day at Camp Grandma, Jake spoke up after all the presentations were done and said, "Hey, everyone, let's all say what we want to be when we grow up. I'll write down your answers."

Katie started, "I want to be a children's book author or a YouTuber."

Jack went next. "I want to be a voice actor or a video game designer or a comic book author."

Then Lauren, nine at the time, spoke up. "From now to thirteen, I want to collect Shopkins. I want to be a surfer person in my teens. In my twenties and thirties, I want to be an actor. In my forties and fifties, I want to work at Great Wolf Lodge. Sometime in my fifties I will start being an artist and continue with that." I had to laugh at the specificity of it all.

Jake said he wanted to become an astronaut and be the first man on Mars.

"Leave it to Jake," said Jack. "He's shooting the highest of all of us, figuratively and literally!"

"Those all sound great! Now, how are you going to get there?"

They looked around the table at each other, then to me. "Go to school?"

"That's a good answer and a good place to start. But here's another," I said. "You plan for it."

START YOUR PLAN

When I was working, we did business plans annually. We usually did those plans at the end of the year so we could start off the New Year with our plans in place. It's a very good practice that many smart businesspeople do to help them be successful. Very simply, on a piece of paper or in a notebook, you write down your goals and what it will take to reach them. Do you have obstacles to overcome? Do you need support or help from others? How will you measure your progress? Those are good things to think about when writing your plan. Then you review your plan throughout the year to make sure you are on track and staying focused. That is how you are assured you will reach your goal.

When I explained this to the kids, their response was typical: "But we are not in business, and we are not grown-ups!"

"That's okay. You don't have to be either one to start planning. It's a good exercise for your mind. It gets you thinking ahead at any age. Think about it as preparing for the future because a plan helps you get where you want to go. A plan helps make your wishes and dreams come true. Let's do one together now.

"We can begin by just describing what you'd like to accomplish next year. School starts soon. What do you hope to achieve in your new grade level? Do you want to make new friends? Do you want to get good grades? Do you want to play a sport or be in a school performance? Just start writing down your intentions and what you would like for next year. Here is a brand-new notebook and pen for each of you to begin. Take your time, no rush."

They started writing without further questions. Finishing, they closed their books and ran off to play—escape at last. Only the oldest, Jack, stayed seated in deep concentration. Finally satisfied, he closed his book and handed it to me.

With all their notebooks in hand, I leafed though, taking stock. Jack (fourteen at the time of this exercise) had fifteen entries, ranging from personal growth to academics and sports. Katie (age eleven) wrote five, including a Christmas gift wish. Jake (age twelve) wanted to get a degree in math (of course, as would any future astronaut), and Lauren (age nine) wrote down five goals, all about relationships and people she cares about.

We would review these a few months later, after they were well into the new school year. We will check the progress and reexamine and modify if need be. These rechecks are important to do periodically. In my working career, I saw too many business plans go into a manager's bottom drawer and never surface again. Not with this grandma! A plan is worthless unless it is revisited. If you are serious about meeting goals, then keep them clearly posted and top of mind. This can motivate you to stay focused on what you want to accomplish.

Do you know what I find amazing? From what I've read and observed, very few people actually write down their goals or do any sort of written plan. This is such a shame. A written plan is like a road map of where you want to go and how you intend to accomplish it step-by-step. It provides focus and clarity and can keep you on track. Why drift? You can get so much more out of life when you plan it with intention.

Another day several months later we were together at Camp Grandma, and as we were doing our agenda, I suggested we add business plans so we could each review and revise our plans, discussing any challenges to overcome. Katie was the facilitator and was writing on the white board. As she finished the agenda, I looked it over.

She had written:

1. Agenda
2. Pep Olympics
3. BBP
4. Brownies
5. Jake's question

I said, "Hey, Katie, what is number three, BBP? I think you forgot business plans."

"No, I didn't," she giggled. "Number three stands for 'boring business plans'!"

LOL (something I learned from them). Okay, I get it. Of course, I never said business plans were exciting, only important. Truth be known, most adults in business would agree with her. I think I'll start calling them boring business plans myself from now on.

ACTIVITY: PLANNING

Call it business planning or life planning, it doesn't really matter. Fundamentally, *planning* is about respecting your time and that of others. Whether you are organizing your activities for the day or your goals in life, understanding that there is only so much time available and wanting to make the most of it is critical to success.

What Kids Will Learn

- Self-respect by learning their time is valuable
- Analytical thinking by identifying what actions will lead to what you want?
- How to set goals
- The concept of time management
- How to self-assess

What You Need

Just paper and pen or pencil for business planning or life planning. For each grandchild you may want to invest in a journal or notebook that he or she can work with on an ongoing basis, adding intentions and goals as the years go by.

A flip chart or chalkboard is fun to use for when you are simply spending time with your grandchildren and want to plan your day. Write out an agenda for your time together. Discussing and planning together gives everyone input—they feel heard—and that makes them invested and more willing to participate in the experience.

What You'll Do

Meeting with your grandchildren one-on-one, sit down together and hand your grandchild a new notebook and pen.

If you feel your grandchildren are old enough to understand, say at least eight or nine years old, then explain that to meet one's goals or help make one's dreams and wishes come true, it helps to write them out.

1. In your own words, explain that stating and writing out *objectives* helps in identifying where you want to be or what you want to accomplish. It provides clarity and gives a person direction.

2. Ask them to write down what *challenges* or obstacles they think they might run into. This is important and will help prepare them for what they may encounter.

3. Ask them to identify what *resources* they think they will need to meet their goals. Might they need help in buying materials? Do they need help with transportation in getting to a special class or lesson?

4. Now, with their focused attention, they can plan a *course of action* or plan of attack. An example: "I want to learn to play the guitar next year. I will commit to practicing every afternoon after school for thirty minutes a day, and I'll ask for lessons for my birthday."

Time Required

An hour or so when you first get started. Although it may be easier to do face-to-face, this can be done over the phone or through written correspondence. The follow-up can be thirty minutes or so, but take as much time as needed to make this a worthwhile activity. If you take it seriously, so will they.

Tips

- This is an activity best suited for children once they start school, ages eight and older. With very young children who can't yet write, you can still start the process. Begin by asking them simple questions like, "What do you want to do now that you are five years old?" Write down their remarks and keep them to review again, maybe when they turn six.
- Keep it simple.
- An easy place to start is at the beginning of a new school year. Ask them what they would like to accomplish in the upcoming year. Then set up a time in your calendar, say every three months, to review with them their entries in their notebooks. Reassessment allows you to

monitor progress and make adjustments as needed.

- Be a role model: share with your grandchildren a plan you did for yourself. Review it with them periodically at the same time you review theirs (a good way to keep you both accountable).
- Planning doesn't always have to be done in a formal manner. In the course of conversation you can help them consider time in a meaningful way by just discussing what you want to accomplish during the time you share together.

For example, I remember the day I took my two granddaughters to Disneyland. In the car I asked them, "What are your favorite rides, and if you could only go on one, what would it be?" From there we worked out a plan for our day, listing the order of our activities based on personal wishes, location within the theme park, and so on. This ensured everyone got to go on their favorite ride or see their favorite attraction, and we had time to eat and shop for souvenirs. My granddaughters did the planning; I just asked the questions.

The day's agenda

CHAPTER THIRTEEN:

THE ANCESTOR WITHIN

After a couple of summers together, Camp Grandma was in full swing. By now I had taken the business themes of teamwork, public speaking, résumés, business planning, and relationship development and modified them to be age appropriate for my grandkids. With the five-year age difference between the oldest and the youngest, I always want each to gain something from the experience, so I have to be flexible and agile, relating the themes to their level. In addition to our more formal exercises, we journal, write poetry, learn about manners, and of course include one or more of the traditional favorites—crafts, cooking, baking, plays, games, songs—as part of our day. While all of these activities feel like fun, these getting-along-in-the-world themes are at the core of our activities together, each of which carries the value of its corporate counterpart. Yet often simply in the course of a day, the opportunity to explore something else important tends to present itself.

"Who's this, Grandma?" Lauren asked one day when looking at a picture of my mother near my bed.

"She is your great-grandmother, my mother."

"Oh, she's pretty!"

"Yes, she was. Would you like to know about her?" And that started the tradition of talking about ancestors, taking time to learn about our family tree.

MY FAMILY TREE

Since my parents did not live long enough to know my grandchildren, I figured who better than me to make the introductions. I always loved hearing stories about my heritage and found it meaningful to know on a larger scale where I came from. Clearly my roots didn't start in California where I was born and neither did my grandchildren's. Kids start off assuming they are the center of the universe, and helping them understand their lineage is one way they can learn that others came before and others will surely follow. They are not alone. Also, it's not unusual for personality and character traits to be passed down, so while we're learning about our ancestors, we might just learn a little about ourselves in the process.

This connection to history and legacy is something of an equalizer between me and my grandkids as well. They see that I had grandparents, too, just as they do. They were surprised to hear that my interest in genealogy started as a child when I had a school project in the sixth grade. I personally interviewed my grandparents, and my nana in California helped me reach out to other distant relatives I never knew I had. She helped me build my family tree, and I have added to it ever since.

They were excited by the idea of an ancestor activity, so I began with my mother. I wanted to keep it simple, so rather than telling her history and putting all four of them to sleep, I decided to pick several small things to know about her that they might actually remember into adulthood.

Toward that end, I considered that people have various learning styles that are most commonly driven by three basic senses: visual, auditory, and kinesthetic. We don't all learn the same way, and while we can expand by training ourselves to learn by a mix of styles, most of us start off with one or two dominant senses that determine how readily we receive information. Those who are more visual respond to seeing pictures, for example. Others whose dominant sense is auditory do better with sound and hearing. Kinesthetic learners are more physical and tactile, using touch or movement as learning tools. Understanding how we perceive most readily can be very helpful, but which senses are dominant in my grandchildren is still emerging to me. To help develop their senses, I try to use all three styles whenever possible.

To present my mother, I put a favorite photo of her on the table. "Let me introduce you to my mother, Mary. She is your great-grandmother," I told them. "Doesn't she have a beautiful smile?" Then we all went out and picked her favorite flower, gardenias (fortunately I grow them and they were in bloom), and we placed them in a vase, also on the table. We passed around the vase so they could smell the fragrance. Afterward, I told them a short story about how she always told the truth because as a very young girl she was caught telling a fib to her mother and had her mouth washed out with soap! She learned the hard way never to tell a lie. We ended our discussion by drawing a picture of gardenias.

In time I want them to know that it was my mother who taught me about unconditional love. Her love was unmatched by any other; she was always selfless, gentle, and giving. My sister says it best: "With Mom, we came before her." She never let her struggles get in the way of caring for her children. By her example, she taught me the power of love, the purpose of love, and ultimately how to love my family.

The next time we did an ancestor activity, the kids met my father, who was a musician. To introduce him I brought out his picture along with his saxophone from storage to let them touch and handle it. They even tried blowing through it, which they learned wasn't easy.

I told them a few facts about my dad: "My father was Italian, and his favorite food was spaghetti with red sauce. His favorite color was blue. He always loved a blue sky." Jack responded, "That's my favorite color," and Jake chimed in, "Mine too." Hearing his music (I had an old recording of it), seeing his picture, and writing down his long, difficult name, Dominic Pasquarelli, cinched the beginning of a connection with him.

Another time they met my grandfather, their great-great-grandfather, Phillippo Pasquarelli, whose story was very interesting to them as he was an immigrant from Italy. We found Italy on the world map and talked about his long voyage across the Atlantic to America. "What did the boat look like, Grandma? What did he eat on the way?"

When I told them he was only seventeen years old, traveling alone as a stowaway and hiding in the bottom of the boat, their eyes opened wide with wonder. I was bombarded with questions then. "What is a stowaway?" "Why didn't he buy a ticket?" "Where were his mom and dad?"

When they learned that he lived from 1886 till 1982, Jake quickly made the observation that he was alive when the *Titanic* sank in 1912. (Jake is my date keeper.)

"Well, it's a good thing he wasn't on the *Titanic,* or we wouldn't be here," Jack observed.

"He could have been on the *Titanic* and been a survivor," Katie suggested.

"I don't think so," Jack said. "I think we would have known about it by now."

Jake confirmed that Phillippo Pasquarelli was not a name on the survivor list (something he personally researched). Glad we got that settled.

There will be many other stories to tell over time as they come to know more about their ancestors. Whenever I tell stories, I try to keep them short and sweet so they can be lasting. I hope that through these shared memories of my parents and my grandparents they may live on in some way. What I've learned is that the love behind that hope is not lost on children.

Now Lauren never passes a gardenia without reminding me that it's my mother Mary's favorite flower, a loving thing to do, which of course makes me happy too. This is not only passing love and tenderness down from one generation to the next but also giving the newest a chance to offer the same right back to the oldest.

ACTIVITY: MEET YOUR ANCESTORS

Introducing family members that are no longer living to your grandchildren can be a rewarding experience on many levels. Kids gain a sense of identity when they learn about family history. Learning about their ancestors can be like learning about themselves. They might recognize similar traits and characteristics in family members that are a match to their own.

What Kids Will Learn

- That they are connected to history
- That past eras, places (geographies), and cultures were different from their own
- That they are not alone
- An appreciation of family legacy
- How to better understand themselves in comparison to others

What You Need

To think of an ancestor that you would like your grandchildren to know. Gather pictures, artifacts, and other memorabilia that may help in telling their story.

What You'll Do

1. Plan an afternoon with your grandchildren or set aside some time together. Remind them of your relationship with them. "You know that I am your grandmother." Then ask, "Would you like to meet my grandmother?" (or mother, father, aunt, uncle, sister, and so on).

2. Then show a picture, tell them the person's name, where he or she lived, and something special or meaningful to you ("I loved my mother's smile"). Try to include all three primary learning styles: visual (something they can see), auditory (hear), and kinesthetic (touch). For instance, use a picture, a fragrance, maybe make a favorite food they can taste, or how about Grandpa's old catcher's mitt and baseball?

3. Suggest they draw a picture reflecting a favorite flower or pet to help reinforce the new information.

Time Required

In preparation, collecting materials and making notes on your ancestor takes a little time. Engaging them in the story may take only an hour or so. Creating a family tree can be an ongoing project lasting months or even years.

Tips

- This is an activity best suited for children once they start school, ages five and older.
- You may also want to start a family tree, filling in the branches together with your grandchildren. There are wonderful templates you can download, print, and use for this purpose.

- From a distance you can still share stories and pictures through the mail and Internet.
- Even though you spend time with your grandchildren, they may not really know much about you. Show them pictures from your youth; share any of your favorites, like color, foods, games, and so on. Believe me, they want to know you too.

Conjuring up the past

CHAPTER FOURTEEN:

RUN WITH YOUR STRENGTHS

Remember in your youth when you got your report card from school? It basically reflected your performance per subject for the preceding semester. You took it home, sometimes pleased to show Mom and Dad, sometimes dreading it. Most of the time it was a mixed bag.

What appeared to be most important to your parents? What grade did they talk most about? Where were you directed to spend more time and invest more energy? You know the answer. It was whatever was the weakest.

Now imagine a world that focused on the As. What would it look like, or feel like, if we focused on our strengths instead of our weaknesses? What I learned in my work-life experience is that our strengths reflect our natural talents and aptitudes. They are our gifts, and too often we fail to capitalize on their value. Maybe it's because they come too easily to us that we minimize their importance. Or maybe because we are good at some things, we think we should be good at all things, so we concentrate on our weaknesses. Or maybe we need to get that good grade in math to get into college.

I'm not suggesting we shouldn't try to overcome our weaknesses or fears. Overall, developing strategies to minimize or manage our flaws can help prevent failure. But when we focus most of our attention on weakness rather than on building on our strengths, we run the risk of wasting precious time and energy that could otherwise help us meet our fullest potential. We sacrifice excellence at one thing for getting better at another.

Not at Camp Grandma. Here, we focus on the As and let the strengths shine.

IDENTIFYING THEIR STRENGTHS

A child's talent can be identified at a young age (sometimes as early as three to five, from what I've been told), and those talents are developed and become strengths between the ages of three to fifteen. So I say let's be a talent scout for our grandchildren and keep on the lookout for their natural talents and tendencies. We can pay attention to how they spend their free time, observing their early curiosities. Do they light up when they hear music? Do they want to move to the rhythm? Are they drawn to animals? Are they readers? Do they write or draw? Do they ask to help you cook or want you to go outside with them to play ball? These are all clues to their interests—which can often develop into strengths—that we can support and reinforce.

In my family, both Lauren and Katie love to sing. But I've also noticed that Lauren writes beautiful poetry and Katie cleverly makes up her own jokes with crafty wordplay. Jake wants to figure out how things are made, and Jack is disciplined and health conscious. Do we have a writer, an entertainer, a builder, or a doctor in training?

I remember when I was in my management role and a top, high producing salesman came to me very frustrated and discouraged. I learned through our conversation that he had lost his focus and felt spread too thin. In reviewing his team structure, it became evident that he was no longer doing what he was best at doing. Instead of developing business, which was what he liked to do, he was caught up managing his team members and overseeing the execution of the business. We found the solution. I suggested he modify the various roles on the team, placing people in positions that focused on their strengths, rather than let tenure or income drive responsibilities. It worked. He went back to selling, and he relinquished the management duties to another. He was much happier once he accepted his strength as his best contribution, and the team ended up better managed.

Our kids don't know their strengths yet. But we can play a key role in nurturing and guiding them along the way. We can help support their natural abilities and aptitudes by providing them lessons or helping locate resources to support their interests, as with tutors, clubs, or organizations. As well, a grandparent can provide varied opportunities and experiences to possibly ignite a spark that might trigger an unrecognized inner passion. If they don't go already, take them to the library, a museum, a cultural festival, or an event. Plan a date to see a musical play or a sporting event. Surprise them with an unexpected outing somewhere, anywhere that can expose them to different ideas and interests. Then see what sticks.

Recognizing his hand-eye coordination and his ability to make good judgments, I asked Jack, "What about golf?"

Jack turned to look at me with the expression of *What are you talking about, Grandma?* He had been feeling rather dejected. Team sports had been a challenge for him, and so far he hadn't found a sport that was a good match to his interests or ability.

"Yes, what about golf?" I repeated. "I can get you some lessons for your birthday." I thought golf might be a good fit for him, something he could play alone or with others, and with the handicap system, he could always have a chance at winning regardless of his ability. And he could play the rest of his life.

That suggestion worked. Jack has taken golf lessons for a year now and likes it a lot. He hopes to make the golf team at school next year, and surprise, he's now taken up basketball too.

WHAT FAILURE CAN TEACH KIDS

The ability to identify people's strengths is an offshoot of recognizing that we are all unique as individuals. The involvement of such a tuned-in grandparent can help kids develop a healthy self-esteem, rather than the "everyone feel good" self-esteem we often see doled out today. Self-esteem should come from within and is the foundation for understanding one's self-worth. Sure, we all want to feel good about ourselves, but we're not all the same, and we can't all win at everything. Understanding our uniqueness and what makes us special gives us a stronger and truer self-image.

Which is why I do not advocate the notion that everyone should get a trophy, or that everyone in the service industry deserves a tip, or that in business just showing up warrants a promotion. Working hard to earn a reward is what gives it meaning. I understand being recognized for doing your best, but somewhere along the way kids have to learn that doing your best may not be good enough. Learning to lose is an important lesson in life that we all have to experience at some point. Yes, losing hurts, but it's important that children understand that there is no shame in failure. The regret will be in not trying. And fortitude and determination are built by trying again once one has failed.

Don't underestimate how aware kids are. They know when they are being patronized. They know who is smarter, who runs the fastest, and who's most popular. They don't need awards and trophies to remind them, and using the trophy-for-all method for recognition, rather than for excellence, can backfire. Though we want to praise and encourage kids along the way, we should avoid false accolades. We certainly don't want them demoralized the first time they fail or to cause them to underachieve in any way. But we do want to properly prepare them for life with a realistic understanding of their strengths and limitations. I recently had the opportunity to hear Kareem Abdul-Jabbar speak at a public event. We know him as the basketball superstar of the '60s, '70s, and '80s. He said something I will never forget. "You can't win unless you learn how to lose." He clearly understands the valuable lessons of defeat.

I encourage my grandchildren not to fear failure. Even when you focus on the As, you won't always win. We all inevitably fail at things. Failure is a part of life and helps us better appreciate when we win. I like to play cards or other games with my grandchildren, and in the beginning I would let them win by not playing my best because I wanted them to build their self-confidence and enjoy the experience. Now I play harder and they are learning to lose, understanding it is all part of the game. Of course their skills are improving as well, so I, too, have to demonstrate being a good sport when losing.

I like to tell my grandchildren stories about Abraham Lincoln and Walt Disney, two famous people they think they know well. "Did you know that Walt Disney was actually fifty-four years old before he experienced success with the opening of Disneyland?" I asked them. "Before that, he suffered from numerous setbacks—bankruptcy, repeated rejections, and emotional breakdowns—but these failures never got in the way of his dreams." And it's even more interesting when I list the failures and defeats that Abraham Lincoln experienced before he became the president of the United States at age fifty-one. "He failed in business, repeatedly was defeated when he ran for Congress and the Senate, had his heart broken when his sweetheart died, and suffered a nervous breakdown. And as president he lost a young son, which was a particularly painful setback. He is a good example of someone who had the courage to overcome obstacles with persistence and perseverance." Failure didn't keep him down for long.

FOCUS ON THEIR STRENGTHS

A grandparent can help their grandchildren embrace the lessons of failure so they can emerge wiser, stronger, and more compassionate and resilient. We can help them understand failure is not the end—it just might be the beginning, an opportunity to set new goals and new priorities—while reinforcing their passions. And the most direct way to get to their passions is through their strengths.

As people who have been there and done that, grandparents can demonstrate how to build on one's innate talents and strengths. We can underscore the importance of developing skills and knowledge, motivating our grandchildren to excel. We can inspire them by our own stories of success, and yes, failure, to try harder and learn to overcome obstacles. We all want our grandchildren to thrive in this world, and a clear appreciation of their strengths as well as their weaknesses can give them a tremendous advantage.

Wouldn't it be great if we all did what we are naturally good at doing and were passionate and excited about doing it? Would we be more productive, more successful? Would we be more motivated, more engaged? Might we be happier living life as we wish? Our grandchildren will have that chance if we encourage them to run with their strengths.

Of course, encouragement is different than applying pressure. I count among my strengths a certain intensity, but I have to modulate that appropriately or it could become a weakness around children. Not to worry, though, if you slip up sometimes or in some ways, your grandchildren will tell you when you do and accept you anyway, as I've learned from Jack.

One of Jack's strengths is his willingness to help others. When we are together he tries hard to please me and I know it. He told me recently, "I like being with you, Grandma, and I don't want to hurt your feelings, but it's exhausting to always be my best around you. It's sometimes good to just be home and play my video games." I had to smile. I get it. I think it's great that he is comfortable telling me that. I actually consider his confession—and the fact that his truth-telling is as much about me as it is about him—another of his strengths.

ACTIVITY: ACCESS YOUR GRANDCHILDREN'S STRENGTHS

We all have strengths and weaknesses. This exercise helps you recognize strengths in your grandchildren that you can then share with them so they too are aware, encouraging them to better understand themselves and make the most of who they are.

What Kids Will Learn

- Self-confidence
- To be more successful
- How to leverage their strengths to be more effective

- To focus their energy on the positives
- Their true potential
- To be happier
- To embrace who they are

What You Need

Time together. A notebook might also be helpful to capture observations and notes.

What You'll Do

1. Observe and follow their interests! Pay special attention, no matter where you are or what you are doing together. Are your grandchildren having fun? Are they excited and engaged or looking off and disinterested? Does the task they are doing come easily to them? Or are they frustrated and struggling? Do they socialize or prefer quiet time alone? Do they offer to help? Are they cooperative, or do they want to take the lead with their own ideas? Interests are often indicators of strengths. There are clues in most situations if you watch carefully.

2. Give feedback: "Oh, I notice you keep your room so neat and tidy." "You are so gentle with the new kitty." "Thank you for being so patient while I finished my shopping." Complimenting and acknowledging their actions or behavior lets them know they are seen and appreciated. As well, it can highlight for them a personal strength.

3. Ask open questions: "What do you like to do best?" "What are your favorite subjects in school?" "What is it about having a new puppy that you think you will like?" As they get older, discuss the concept of strengths/weaknesses and ask what they perceive theirs to be. You might start with asking, "What comes naturally to you?"

4. Help them build on their strengths. Support, support, support. If your grandchild has an interest or talent, help with lessons or experiences. Get them the tools they need to succeed. Encourage them and praise their efforts.

Time Required

Anytime you are together

Tips

- Be open-minded. Don't just look for strengths that you want them to have. And don't try to force an interest on them. You are learning about a new person, your grandchild, and you are discovering together what is unique and special about them.
- Be careful not to stereotype. They are growing and changing all the time. It's best to go with the flow. If they have an interest at four years old, don't be surprised if by eight they don't feel the same way about it. Grandparents can encourage experimentation. We can suggest new activities and interests and expose them to new ideas, giving them time and space to explore and discover more about themselves.

You might want to download an exercise that I saw on the website Understood.org. It is a printable activity written by Amanda Morin called "Hands-on Activity to Identify Your Child's Strengths." It looks like fun to me!

Jack frosting a cake (he's good at making bagels too!)

CHAPTER FIFTEEN:

REPUTATION AND TECHNOLOGY

"Who can tell me what a reputation is?" I asked the kids at a recent Camp Grandma day.

Now that they are all older, I can introduce more mature concepts and trust we will have a meaningful conversation. By this point I have been doing Camp Grandma for five years. Many of the themes I've raised over the years are now being discussed at home with their parents or in school. So I like that I can reinforce the topics and provide a platform where we can freely share perspectives.

BUILDING A GOOD REPUTATION

They all knew what a reputation is, but it was Katie, age twelve at this point, who nailed it. "It's what others think of you from observing your behavior." We went on to talk about how you build a positive reputation, and they all shared.

"Don't lie."

"Don't gossip about your friends."

"Stay out of jail."

"Don't strangle people." (Art Linkletter was right years ago when he said, "Kids say the darndest things!")

"Be known for something awesome!"

We discussed the traits of a good reputation, starting with good character. They all contributed to create a long list that included being helpful, grateful, kind, loyal, responsible, trustworthy, and caring. Jack contributed, "With good morals and intentions." Jake added, "Being wonderful." I think they got it.

Then I brought out their journals and asked them to write down answers to these questions:

What do you think your reputation is now?

What do you want to be known for?

What can you do to change your reputation?

When they were finished, we went around the table and they shared their answers about themselves and discussed each other's reputations. It was a lively exchange, clearly showing that they understood the value of a good reputation.

I emphasized that their reputation was actually their most valuable possession and that they needed to maintain and protect it. The topic led us to the Internet. Here I have to compliment moms, dads, and teachers, too, because I was pleased to see that my grandchildren had already been cautioned about how the Internet can hurt a reputation.

Though my grandchildren are now only texting with their friends, it won't be long before they will be participating in other technologies. I was glad to hear they'd already had a heads-up as to the pitfalls that lie ahead from misuse of social media. Though I didn't have to deal with this growing up or while raising my own kids, my grandchildren will have to accept that their future posts on Facebook, their tweets, and other Internet exchanges could haunt them forever. They must always be mindful and practice both discretion and restraint.

I suggested they ask themselves, *Do I really want the world to see this? Can I really count on a friend to not forward my picture or secret to someone else? What if my parents saw this, or, gulp, Grandma? Though I may feel strongly about something now (like hurt or anger), do I want to take the chance that this could be broadcast out to everyone, defining me like this forever?*

THE CHALLENGES OF TECHNOLOGY

Clearly, managing technology will require ongoing effort, not just in protecting your reputation on social media but also in understanding and keeping up with all the new innovations and opportunities available with tech products. I trust my grandchildren will learn to handle it all just fine. They're already so much better at it than I am.

I must confess that I am frequently challenged by technology. I just learn how to operate one device and a new version comes out, and I have to start all over. My computer breaks down, and I am helplessly out of business until I can get help. I forget my phone when going out and literally feel disconnected from the world.

To say that I struggle with technology is putting it mildly. I have come kicking and screaming into the twenty-first century. I'm old-fashioned; I like the anticipation of letters in the mail. I like the feel and smell of a real book in my hands. I prefer communicating with others face-to-face, both verbally and nonverbally. And I like to feel like I have someone's full attention when together, without being constantly pinged and buzzed.

Okay, I'll admit there are elements of technology I have learned to love. I love the convenience of information at my fingertips. I love to Skype with my sister-in-law who lives abroad, feeling as if we are in the same room together. I love my Bluetooth, so I can stay in contact with friends while I drive. I love my smartphone and all it provides in such a compact package, continually amazing me. I also love getting texts from my grandchildren and knowing we are spending the "moment" together. True, I liked when life was simpler, but let's face it, technology and the digital world are here to stay, so I need to get with the program.

Like a lot of parents and grandparents, I have been concerned about the influence of technology on young lives with both its positive and negative effects. Now that I have a grandchild who's a teenager, I'm paying more attention. I know his generation is entrenched in technology, and I'm troubled by the loss of human connection. I worry about the risks of social networking and addiction to gaming, not to mention the hours I see lost in deep concentration on a device. I ask, "Why don't you go outside and play with your friends?" Then I remember kids don't do that anymore. They have playdates instead. I know his parents, like so many others, have been working with him to set time limits and to find a balance that works for their family. I appreciate their challenge, one my parents never had when I was growing up. Well, as they say, "If you can't beat them, join them." I decided that to stay relevant and closer to my grandchildren as they grow older, I'd better understand how they use technology. So I asked Jack for his help.

Clueless when it comes to video games, I am now the student. He is patiently showing me how they work and bringing me into his world, even introducing me to his online friends (unbelievable!). Katie is getting into the act, too, by teaching me about Minecraft. This should be easy enough to learn, except for my dozing off during her demonstrations. Sigh. "Wake up, Grandma!" she exclaimed. "You missed a good part." She was so kind to repeat it!

Lauren has discovered apps as well. No matter where we are, at any given moment she informs me of the wait times for attractions at Disneyland. "Guess what, Grandma? There is a 120-minute wait for the Peter Pan ride!" she breathlessly announced while we were shopping one day. Amazing. How did I ever get along without all this before?

Hard as this is for me to digest, it is important to know because it is important to them. If I want them to take an interest in me and my life and to feel needed (as I do by them), then it is only right that I reciprocate.

BALANCING TECHNOLOGY

It's a given that technology and social media will continue to play a big role in their lives. Keeping it under control will be the challenge. With any luck, I might serve as a counteracting influence to the technological connections. Since I am the last generation of folks not raised with technology, maybe I can keep them from letting technology saturate their lives. I can remind them that online life is not real life and that they need to regularly step away from their devices and experience the physical world. I can encourage them to walk with their eyes looking straight ahead and all around to take in the present moment, embracing the here and now.

I can show them how to interact socially with each other rather than at arm's length when online through gaming and other social media. I can remind them that if they rely on technological connections they will miss the human connection. I won't have any trouble saying, "Please put away your technology for the time being. Talk to each other. Sit down and have a face-to-face conversation. Don't hide behind your electronic screen. Get to really know one another and develop a genuine and caring relationship . . . starting with me."

I think nature can help too. Certainly nature is a strong antidote to technology. Nature offers the brain a break. Experiencing less stress and a quieter environment gives us a lift, helping us to be more creative, take a breath, contemplate, and let our minds wander. Jack recently told me one of his favorite memories is going to the mountains because he feels peaceful there. That's a good thing.

And though not everyone can visit the mountains, we can encourage our grandchildren to pay better attention to the sky or a flower or a cool breeze.

My hope is that my grandchildren will avoid the addiction to mobile devices that affects so many kids today. At the very least I can help do my part in keeping it all in balance, encouraging them to use their brains in different ways to counter the ever greater demands of the digital world.

"Grandma, I'm bored," Lauren said one day. "Can I use your iPad?"

"Not now. Why don't you read a book?"

"I don't want to 'cause it makes me sleepy in the daytime."

"Well, I have to admit, it does for me too."

"So can we play cards?"

"Sure, how about Old Maid?"

"Okay. Can I win?"

"Only if you play the game better than I do."

And speaking of things that feel beyond our control, here's one more thing to consider: information overload. Katie says she doesn't listen to the news. I asked her why and she answered, "Because ignorance is bliss." Hard to argue with that.

ACTIVITY: VALUING YOUR REPUTATION

Teaching your grandchildren about the value of reputation can appreciably influence how they mature as adults. Help them understand that creating their own identity is within their control. This, in and of itself, is empowering and ensures they live a life of intention.

What Kids Will Learn

- The importance of reputation
- That reputation is the opinion others have of them based on observing their behavior
- That they are in control of their reputation
- How to maintain and protect their reputation

What You Need

Quiet time to engage in this thoughtful discussion. Provide paper or notebook and pen so you can capture their comments. You might want to prepare for your discussion by writing down several questions for them to answer once you have made your introduction.

What You'll Do

1. Start by asking them if they understand the concept of "reputation," then listen carefully and respond by clarifying and teaching.

2. Explain to your grandchildren that a reputation is "your actions plus what others say about you."

3. Ask them, "What is your reputation now?"

4. Ask them, "What would you like to be known for?"

5. Then discuss responses.

6. Something else you might like to do is write down the reputations of other family members, or celebrities or sports figures, to get them thinking about positive and negative reputations.

7. Talk about ways to hurt a reputation and how they must be careful with technology.

8. For older children, ask: "Are you your reputation?" "Do you care what others think about you?" "Should we care about our reputation?" Entering into discussions about how a reputation can influence future employment opportunities and meaningful relationships can remind them of the importance of creating a great impression in real life.

Time Required

At least an hour to begin with, then fifteen minutes or so from time to time to keep the topic top of mind and relevant.

Tips

- This exercise works best with grandchildren ages ten and older.
- From a distance, this is certainly a conversation you can have with your grandchildren once you have developed an open and trusting relationship.
- Oh, and you might want to suggest they not brag about themselves: "Show people, don't tell them."

Jake—our very own astronaut

CHAPTER SIXTEEN:

UNLEASHING YOUR SELF-EXPRESSION

I was first introduced to Flat Stanley in March of 2013, when Jake was in the fourth grade. Flat Stanley is a paper cutout character that kids in Jake's fourth-grade class were asked to carry around with them for a week. Every night, as a homework assignment, they had to write five sentences describing the adventures and experiences of Flat Stanley.

I noticed this assignment on the table and read Jake's entry about Flat Stanley:

> He likes going to Granada.
> He likes going to work.
> He likes the playground.
> He likes going to the library.
> He loves Grandma.

I was touched. This was the first time Jake had expressed his feelings for me in words. Communicating his emotions isn't particularly easy for him to do, as is true for many children, so thank goodness for Flat Stanley. The Flat Stanley literacy project is a popular activity for elementary students. It's based on a 1964 children's book written by Jeff Brown about a little boy who is flattened in his sleep by a bulletin board. After the students read the book and become familiar with the story line, they are asked to create their own paper Flat Stanley and take him around with them for a week, journaling his adventures and experiences. For kids like Jake, Flat Stanley apparently offers an indirect and more accessible way to express themselves.

SELF-EXPRESSION COMES IN MANY FORMS

Self-expression is critical to childhood development. I know that children who are encouraged to engage in self-expression gain self-confidence, display individuality, and learn to cope with their feelings.

Children must be able to express what they feel or need, and it is easier for them to do so in an environment that feels safe. Camp Grandma offers an opportunity for them to practice self-expression in an open yet protected setting.

All of our activities at Camp Grandma allow for self-expression in one way or another as the kids are encouraged to speak up for themselves, whether through show and tell, giving voice on a team, or in cooperative play. And though learning communication skills is bedrock to our time together, one of the best ways kids express themselves is through creative arts. We do plenty of that at Camp Grandma too.

In addition to their dress-up plays, dance performances, and other team activities, there is plenty of time for individual creativity in the form of painting, drawing, coloring, writing, and building. I keep a well-stocked craft cabinet with the basics like paper, crayons, markers, glue, paints, and scissors, and I like to visit the local hobby store to bring home surprises for the kids, like unpainted birdhouses for them to decorate. Shaving cream and clay are staples in my closet as well. One of the kids' favorite pastimes is sculpturing, and I have been pleasantly surprised as I've watched them create and let their imaginations run wild—they've made moon landscapes out of shaving cream and the cutest penguins out of clay.

One day Jack, Katie, and I were at the beach. We collected rocks of various shapes and sizes. Then, at our next Camp Grandma with all the kids together, we took the rocks and added plastic eyeballs, scraps of fabric, yarn, and glitter and made rock monsters! Easy, inexpensive, and another chance for them to express themselves through artistic means.

By allowing children to experience art in their own way, we learn how they see the world around them and how they think and feel. They are expressing themselves in their own unique way and reveal themselves to me unfiltered and unscripted.

"Look at me dance, Grandma!" Lauren would often exclaim as she twirled around the room.

"Would you like to see my latest drawing, Grandma?" Jack asks with drawing in hand.

"Grandma, see the dress I sewed for my doll!" says Katie as she hands me her rag doll.

And as I walk in the family room, I notice a village Jake had just finished building out of Legos.

Wow! I love it all: the dance, the drawing, the dress, the Lego project. And I love to see what interests them and gets them excited.

When they express themselves, it gives me an insight into each of them, not just as they are when together as cousins at Camp Grandma but also as individuals. I know how they behave. I know their interests, their likes and dislikes, what they eat, their sleep patterns, and their daily schedules. I honor each for their differences and what makes them unique. I am always able to take the time and make the effort to modify whatever we do to suit their particular needs. They are not treated the same, but they are always treated as equals.

I love what they contribute of themselves within the accepting atmosphere Camp Grandma has created. Sometimes they are serious, sometimes playful, and sometimes quirky. Sometimes they appear freer to me when we are together, without Mom or Dad. The difference is subtle but noticeably less restrained. This makes sense because of the children's strong desire to always please their parents.

I asked Jack one day, "How come you are different with me when Mom and Dad aren't here?"

He said, "It's because you are Grandma!" That made perfect sense to him and was a good enough reason for me.

ACTIVITY: ENCOURAGING SELF-EXPRESSION

Kids are born as unique individuals. Self-expression comes naturally to them until they are taught to rein it in and act in certain ways. So though they will grow up and adhere to more conventional means of expression, we should encourage them not to ever lose their inner child and their ability to express their deepest thoughts, feelings, and opinions.

What Kids Will Learn

- How to connect and interact with others
- That we are different from anyone else— and that's okay!
- To be viewed as individuals
- Problem-solving skills
- How to cope with feelings
- Communication skills
- Self-confidence—as a result of being seen and heard
- How to distinguish themselves from others

What You Need

Materials to encourage creativity:

1. Paper or a journal and a pencil for writing

2. Crayons and coloring books for coloring

3. Blocks and/or Legos for building

4. Craft supplies for creative projects including colored construction paper, glue, scissors, scraps of fabric, pipe cleaners, glitter, paints, clay, shaving cream, and so on

5. Dress-up clothes or costumes for acting

6. Music for dancing and singing

7. An inexpensive eight-by-ten-inch picture frame or cardboard cut-out frame

What You'll Do

When spending time with your grandchild or grandchildren:

1. Suggest craft projects that might interest them to do either together or on their own—like painting, sculpturing, drawing, and building.

2. Hand them a journal or a notepad along with a pencil and ask them to write you a story or poem, provided they are old enough to read and write. If they are younger in age, then suggest they draw you a picture.

3. Encourage conversation. Ask them how they are feeling or what they think about a topic. Try to get a dialogue going so they learn to express themselves verbally.

4. Play music when you are together. Get up and dance! Or sing!

5. Using an empty picture frame (without glass) or cardboard cutout frame, hold it up to their face and ask them to make faces that emulate emotions. Make a game out of identifying the expression (sad, happy, fearful, joyful, etc.).

6. Dress up and act out a story together.

Time Required

Usually only an hour or two is all it will take to do any of these activities. Varying the experiences would probably require numerous get-togethers, but that's the fun of it!

Tips

- Model self-expression through your own words and actions. Express yourself when together with your grandchildren. Let them know how you are feeling, what you care about, and how you think about various subjects.
- Be alert to behavior that reflects their individuality and acknowledge it. Let them know they are being seen and heard.
- You don't always need a dedicated time allowed for many of these activities. Use what time you have. For instance, when waiting in the doctor's office, pull out a piece of paper and a pen and ask them to draw a picture. Or when baking cookies, suggest they use chocolate chips or icing to draw faces that describe their feelings.

Katie and Lauren having fun expressing themselves

PART 3.
LESSONS LEARNED

Sharing the love

CHAPTER SEVENTEEN:

WHAT WE CAN ALL LEARN FROM THE BEARDED DRAGON

One afternoon I went to pick up Lauren from summer school. She was eight years old at the time and came running out breathlessly to tell me she had learned about bearded dragons in her reptile class and wanted one for a pet. I told her she would have to ask Mom and Dad. When Mom came home to the question and sweetly replied, "I don't think so . . . not now," I thought that was the end of it. Not quite.

Later that evening I retrieved a voice message on my phone from Lauren. I saved it, and here is what she said:

"Hi, Grandma! What would you say if we could keep the bearded dragon at your house in the kids' room? Mom doesn't want it at our house, so I thought I would ask if it could come to your house. I'll come feed it every week and give it a bath once a month. I'll take good care of it. I know it eats vegetables and sleeps in a large crate with a shoebox when he is in the car. If it is a girl, we can call her Jewel, and if it is a boy, Mike. And it could belong to all the grandchildren so they wouldn't be left out. I talked to my friend who has one, and she told me all about them. I made notes. Please respond. Love, Lauren."

I was amazed. Actually dumbfounded. In that one message she worked her negotiating skills, identifying the obstacle and problem-solving, then listing solutions and benefits. Then she asked for the order. Wow! Camp Grandma might be working too well.

All along I'd intended to pass on what I'd learned in my life to lend my grandchildren a head start in theirs. Yet this many years into Camp Grandma and still I was learning too, learning from my grandkids. I was reminded of the childlike qualities within us that are at the heart of being successful in life, personally and professionally. If we lose them in adulthood, our grandchildren can help us regain them. There are quite a few things we can learn from children. (Corporate America, are you listening?) There's a case to be made for that bearded dragon, as Lauren demonstrated—that raw authenticity that once came naturally to us. Playful, hopeful, imaginative, curious; surely in the working world, we could find a way to accommodate those natural ways of being.

KIDS TEACH US

Here are just a few of the lessons we can learn from our grandchildren.

Believe Anything Is Possible

We are born creative thinkers in the making, and when we are young and inexperienced we enjoy the advantage of dreaming big. But as adults, we frequently have to be reminded to *think outside the box* because we have learned to limit ourselves. By focusing only on the obvious, what we have come to know and expect, we set our own roadblocks, convinced we will fail before we even begin. But what if we took some cues from children and were open-minded and daring enough to think big? We could actually change our reality. We start by simply believing we can.

I get to the believing part through visualization. What is the old adage? Seeing is believing. I remember as a young girl imagining myself as a cheerleader. I saw myself in the outfit and in front of the bleachers long before I actually was. And when my husband and I found a house we loved (way out of our price range), I saw myself in the home, living there. Four years later it was ours, not by some magic but by establishing a goal and picturing ourselves in the future. There is power in our thoughts and imagination, and in believing anything is possible. Children are something of a role model to us, a reminder that human beings are born to harness that power for good and make dreams a reality.

Be Honest and Authentic

One day I went to open the front door for Jack and his family. It just so happened I was wearing an apron. Jack came in and whispered in my ear, "That's *not* a good look for you, Grandma." I don't think I've worn an apron since.

You never know what children are going to say because their thoughts remain unfiltered until they're socialized to be polite, circumspect, and so forth. My grandchildren are unaware of the "PC police," and they speak from their hearts. They already know not to be disrespectful or make hurtful or rude remarks, yet they speak truthfully without fear of censorship or judgment. I treasure their freedom of expression and prize their authenticity. In an effort to be more empathetic and sensitive, I'm afraid we adults are sometimes guilty of overcorrection and control our messages to the extreme.

We walk a fine line to be courteous, thinking surely there is a way to be forthright while remaining civil. There is value in learning the social graces and even more value in balancing them with honesty and authenticity, which creates trust.

This directly relates to reputation. From my years in business, I learned that your reputation is all you really have at the end of the day. And a good reputation is trust maintained consistently over a long period of time. Others remember you for your integrity, ethics, and moral standards more than they do for any title you achieved or money you received.

One of my proudest moments came when I worked for the Yellow Pages selling advertising. In the same year

I earned both the Top Producer Award for the company nationwide for having the highest sales volume and also simultaneously earned its President's Award, honoring the sales associate with the lowest decrease and cancellation rates along with the lowest complaint rate. To win both awards at the same time—highest sales along with lowest errors and complaints—was a first in the company. It had never happened before.

So the idea that you can't play by the rules and get ahead is a cop-out. Sure it takes hard work, perseverance, and commitment to be successful. But let's not forget how we started out as kids when we weren't conditioned to be anything else but honest and authentic. By combining all these behaviors, you are sure to like who you see in the mirror looking back.

Ask More Questions

Children ask a lot of questions, and we can learn something from that. How many of us think we know all the answers when, in fact, we don't even know what questions to ask? What happens to our curiosity as we get older? Children remind us that curiosity is a form of vitality we need to retain. Curiosity can lead you to developing empathy and compassion as well if you listen attentively to the answers your questions solicit.

Even outside of a learning or business environment, asking the right question is a basic skill in good communication and can help not only in gaining information but also in building stronger relationships. How many times have you been with a group of people and left the experience without even one person asking about you, your job, or your family? Now turn that around and remember how you felt when someone asked you questions and actually expressed an interest in you. It made a difference, right? We might all be better off if we were more curious and asked more questions. I actually credit my success in sales and management to my ability to front-load my interactions with clients and colleagues with questions.

There is a modification to the Golden Rule *(Do unto others as you would have them do unto you)* that I've come to prefer after spending time with my grandchildren, and it's *Do unto others as* they *would have you do unto* them. Instead of thinking about behavior based on our own perspective (needs or wants), change the focus to others. Treat people not as you want to be treated but as they want to be treated. Consider what might be important to them and act accordingly. If you don't know, then ask more questions. We can be authentic without being rude or abrasive. We can take a stand and express ourselves but be mindful that others may see it differently. If we can be more open and respectful of our differences, whether they're cultural or political, we might come to better understand ourselves and the world in which we live.

I learned a valuable lesson in school when I was on the debate team (which gives me an idea for another Camp Grandma activity). We were given a topic but not told what side of the debate we would address until the day of the contest. We had to be able to argue either side. I love this. We really have no right to a position on anything without understanding the other side, do we? Children have it all over us on this one because they ask questions all the time.

So when you feel bombarded by questions from your grandchildren, stop and value the importance of what they are doing. They are seeking information and learning to listen, to weigh and assess the answers, and to accommodate diversity. Curiosity and asking questions could become a valuable lifelong habit. We would be wise to follow their lead by asking them a question or two.

Be an Objective Listener

The other half of asking questions is actually the more important half, and children win hands down on this one too. Objectivity is one advantage of childhood; carrying very little baggage, children start off open-minded and nonjudgmental. They don't have preconceived notions regarding the messages they are receiving, nor do they stubbornly hold on to their own position or opinion when they stand corrected. There is no ego to contend with at a young age. Hallelujah! Being a good listener is essential if you want to be a good leader—or a good anything else for that matter.

Just listening at all is a start these days. Is it my imagination or are adults listening less and less? I suspect it is a consequence of the pace we lead, continually pressed to work and move faster, technology driving our momentum. We're growing increasingly impatient, whether driving in traffic or waiting for a slow Internet connection. No one has time. No one has a moment to waste. So is it any surprise that we interrupt when someone is talking and finish the person's sentences (since we assume we know what will be said next)?

Maybe that's another reason I like to spend time with my grandchildren. It is great to have a conversation with them—they actually wait to hear what I will say next.

Be Vulnerable

Nothing is as strong as vulnerability. No improvement or advancement is possible unless we have the courage to take risks, tell hard truths, and admit to lack of knowledge or a mistake we made. Children live with open hearts and embrace vulnerability. They have no image to protect. Spending time with my grandchildren has reminded me of this.

Being vulnerable is an opportunity for growth. Getting past our hang-ups in feeling we always have to be strong and confident, we can open ourselves to what is possible. People regard us as stronger when we share our fears and challenges, when we ask for and receive help from others, and when we take responsibility for missteps and apologize. This is because vulnerability takes courage and a level of self-confidence. Children are brave until we unintentionally give them millions of reasons not to be.

"Hey, Grandma, keep up!" the kids call out as we walk down the street. I quicken my pace, glad for the prompt (people pay good money to an exercise coach for this service). I shift my focus from my arthritic knees and move faster to catch up. Feeling the burn—just another benefit of hanging out with the young.

CHAPTER EIGHTEEN:

THE VIEW FROM THE BALCONY

Everybody knows it's harder to be a parent than a grandparent. As a grandparent you can rest between visits and live your own life. You're not with your grandchildren all the time, and even if you are, you're not carrying the primary responsibility. That's an advantage.

But there's another plus that creates a storehouse of rewards for grandparents, and that's our vantage point. Observing our grandchildren is like viewing from the balcony, and what a view! Our perspective is so clear; we see the whole person, their nature, their character.

Parents sit closer, supervising, correcting, and directing each move. *(Stand still, don't forget your manners, go to bed, wake up, clean your room, finish your vegetables,* and so on.) Parents do the real work, full-time, 24/7. They carry the primary load of raising children from infancy to adulthood, personally (and financially) supporting their physical, emotional, social, and mental development. Whew! But watching our grandchildren from a distance, with space and time in between, gives us a different appreciation of the individual. I learn a great deal from my observations and from spending time with them. Camp Grandma has changed me. Here are some more lessons I've learned:

LIVE IN THE PRESENT

With few exceptions, I never lived in the present before my grandchildren came along. I was always revisiting, reliving, reviewing, and reminiscing about the past, or planning, goal setting, visualizing, and working for some point in the future. What a joy to live in the moment! My grandchildren captivate me; I can patiently watch them for hours—their appearance and mannerisms, their expressions, their movements. I see glimpses of recognizable DNA: their parents, my father, my mother, my grandparents, but in a new and unique person. I see bits of me as I was in my youth, and I can relive those times in the present. I learn about myself from observing the ways we are both alike and different.

What struck me first at Camp Grandma is that I don't move the way I used to (when I was younger), but they sure do. I watch my grandchildren in constant movement, and it brings back memories of the energy, physical strength, and stamina in me that I took for granted as a young girl. There is never an idle moment for them, either physically or mentally. Even when they are quiet, their brains are working, focused on the task at hand, be it coloring and writing or just running about. Oh, how I wish I had that energy now! And actually, I do have some of it back now, just from being around them.

I also marvel at their innocence. They are so trusting. The wisdom of my years doesn't quite substitute for the beauty in their open and less skeptical natures. There is authenticity in everything they do. I'd like to tap into the tender heart I, too, once had. They remind me of how it feels to be unguarded and enthusiastic about the simplest things in life. I now try to see things through their eyes and take a fresh look at what I may have been missing. I know this sounds trite, but they awaken my inner child. I experience many things again as if for the first time when I am with them. Who thought Disneyland could be so much fun again?

It seems I pay more attention to everything now, like eating a snow cone on a hot summer day or feeling the beat of a song and jumping up to dance whenever I feel like it. As if relishing the comfort of a cool breeze, I am more mindful of each moment, less on autopilot in their company. In requiring my attention, which I am so happy to give, they remind me to pay attention to other happy things too.

I can honestly say that for the first time, in the company of my grandchildren, I have learned to live in the present. They are wonderful role models for me.

CARE LESS WHAT OTHERS THINK

Caring less about what others think is a load off my shoulders. Parents of young children are often judged by the behavior of their children—or misbehavior, as the case may be. They get that judgmental glare of disapproval from others that says, *Can't you control your child?* This can feel to the mom or dad like people think they're a lousy parent. When my children were young, I was sensitive to what others thought of my parenting. I bought into the belief that children were a reflection of their parents. Well, the fact is that's not necessarily so.

When children have a mind of their own or have some developmental issue going on, they can't always behave as adults wish them to. Circumstances may be beyond their control. If and when my grandchildren behave badly (crying or being disruptive on occasion when they were younger), I tune out other people unless they offer to help. I focus all my energy on my grandchild who needs my attention. I try to mitigate the situation as quickly as possible, sometimes leaving the place, so as to not disturb others, but now I do that out of courtesy and not because I fear others' judgment. I no longer feel performance anxiety. I also try extra hard not to judge others as quickly, especially without knowing the details. I realize that the subtle, and sometimes not so subtle, critiques of parenting abilities by others can be painful, but fortunately not to me anymore. What a relief.

DISENGAGE FROM THE OUTCOME

Is our development determined by heredity or life experiences? As a parent, I believed in nurture over nature, and hoped that I could mold and shape my children as I saw fit. But as I watched my children grow up, I began to reconsider my position. Now with the time I have spent with my grandchildren, I tend to favor the nature theory. It almost seems that they come into the world as they were meant to be—with maybe a few adjustments. We can certainly influence and give guidance, but I don't believe you can change a person's nature. Your best bet is not to even try.

Instead, at Camp Grandma I prefer to work to understand who they are and bring out their best traits. I support and nourish their interests and passions rather than ask them to adhere to any preconceived notion I may have as to their outcome. This is about acceptance, not trying to change people. An Ayurvedic doctor that I see regularly, who is Hindu and also a friend, once gave me this example of how to manage people. "Consider a mountain; you're not going to move it. You'll appreciate it for what it is and find ways to get around it or over it or through it, but it remains a mountain, as it should. You can learn about that mountain, see its beauty, and experience what it has to offer. It's the same with people."

He went on to give me good advice. "Do the best you can and let go. Disengage from the outcome. You are not in charge of how they turn out." I can understand this now, but I don't think I would have accepted that as a young parent. Then I felt the future of my children was under my control. I was too focused on the results of my parenting, willing to take credit for their brilliance or assuming the blame for any failure. I'm so glad I see things differently now. I like my seat in the balcony.

In my family I saw immediate differences between my four grandchildren. Jack and Lauren are pleasers, outgoing, and social; Jake and Katie quieter, more content to play alone. One is highly sensitive and artistic, one a caretaker and people manager, another very creative and cooperative, and the other very intellectually focused and marching to his own drummer.

This isn't to say they don't share many characteristics; it's just that some characteristics are more dominant. I vividly remember an outing with Lauren (our caretaker) when she was just three years old. Lauren, her brother Jake, and I were at a local market and bakery. It was a bit crowded at the bakery counter, so after they pointed to the donuts they wanted, I asked them to go sit at a table nearby (where I could see them) and wait for me while I paid. Jake promptly found a table and sat down.

What I saw next was amazing. Lauren went to the table next to Jake and began dragging a chair over to where he was sitting. At first I didn't understand what she was doing. Then I got it. Without saying a word, she immediately recognized there were only two chairs at the table Jake chose. She then took it upon herself to make sure I had a chair too. Even many adults don't think to do that, but here was a three-year-old excited to get her chocolate donut, yet with the presence of mind to notice a chair was missing and that I would need one. She did it automatically and never mentioned it. If I hadn't been watching them and seen with my own eyes what she did, I would have assumed the third chair was already there.

Was she born that way?

Dominant tendencies and inborn traits are what make children unique and who they are. I don't know how they got them, but I do know that such personality traits were noticeable practically from the moment they were born. I came to acknowledge this more fully as I grew as a grandmother.

Nature versus nurture? There is no way to forecast the development or the outcome of an individual's life. All I hope to do as a grandparent is offer my best traits in their presence and to appreciate them for who they are.

BE YOURSELF

Something else I've learned from spending alone time with my grandchildren is how it feels to be free, to be completely myself. I don't have to pretend or meet others' expectations. With my grandchildren I am comfortable in their open and loving company to express myself, act out in funny ways, sing and dance when I feel like it—although all of them are quick to remind me not to do it in public. (Other than that, I have no PC police looking over my shoulder.) I don't have to impress anyone with my résumé or worry about how my hair looks or whether I'm dressed fashionably. They accept me for the person I am and actually like me for it (even if I do have "coffee breath" sometimes, as Lauren points out). Lucky me.

With them, I find I laugh out loud more often. I remember vividly when Jack was very young, getting him buckled in his car seat was always a challenge for me. I would be leaning over, fumbling around, and he would start laughing at my ineptitude. That of course would get me going, and before I knew it we were both cracking up! It was so nice not having to make excuses for myself or to defend my lack of experience. I struggled doing it, and it was just plain funny. Although I'm much better at managing car seats now, I still laugh at the memory.

Getting along with adults requires more finesse and diplomacy, and as a people pleaser I tend to suspend some aspects of my personality depending on the people I'm with. Maybe that will change as I continue to revel in being who I am more and more with the grandkids. It's quite relaxing and enjoyable, really, to feel free to be more myself regardless of the context.

LET GO

To love so completely and yet be able to let go can be one of the hardest things in the world. If you spend a lot of time with your grandchildren and help with childcare, you are deeply involved in their daily schedule; you know what they eat, when they sleep, poop, play, and so on. You are in their lives so fully, and then you must part at the end of the day. Even though you are ready to go and return to your life, it can be painful to disengage. But you go because you know they are not yours.

My daughter-in-law shows her compassion for this, I think, as she frequently texts me with pictures of the children and stories about what they are doing when I'm not with them. This is her saying to me, *We're okay and we're thinking of you too.* This is very thoughtful and sweet of her to do. I am so grateful. Without my saying anything, she understands my separation anxiety and how much I miss them.

FEEL THE LOVE

What else have I learned as a grandma? I've learned to recognize all the special ways people can say *I love you* without saying a word:

Experiencing the complete joy of Lauren running into my arms when I used to pick her up from preschool and her ongoing trust that I will always be there to "catch" her.

The comfort in knowing that even as a teenager, Jack still wants to spend time with me. Recently he asked that we "stay in touch and hang together more often." As if he had to ask.

The delight in hearing Katie always rush to open the door when I arrive and greet me with her loving smile and big hug.

And the feeling of belonging when I first see Jake. He barely looks up at me when I walk in the door, as if to say, *No big deal. Grandma's here, as she should be.*

CHAPTER NINETEEN:

GRANDPARENTING 101

Being a good grandma or grandpa is surprisingly easy. All you have to do is show up. So as amazing as I think Camp Grandma is for kids—mentoring them, teaching them life skills, learning from them in return— you don't have to do it as formally as I do to be successful. First and foremost, the role of a grandparent is that of the loving responder, and as long as you're responding lovingly to what presents itself in the moment, you're doing it right.

I think some view grandparenting as a second chance at parenting, an opportunity to improve on mistakes you may have made as a parent. Respectfully, I disagree. I view the roles as entirely different, like apples and oranges. Although some grandparents have to parent if they have full-time care of their grandchildren, that is not the case for most of us.

OUR ROLES

I am still a parent to my daughter and son, and I notice that I function much differently as a grandparent. The generational divide changes the focus for me. There is no risk that my grandchildren view me as a substitute mom or dad. Moms are moms; dads are dads. I am Grandma, an entirely different species altogether. I have different responsibilities and come from a different place.

What I do share with my grandchildren's parents is unconditional love for their children. This allows us to get past any differences we may encounter along the way. We share the intention of doing what is best for the children. It's not a contest of parenting styles. It's important to always remember that they are the parent and in charge. I am the grandparent and am there to support, mentor, teach, and provide context within the family.

Restating the obvious, grandparents are not the parents. Parents are powerful; they have the ability to protect, provide for, and prepare their children for adulthood. Parents can punish, teaching the child consequences to unwanted behavior. Parents play the key role in forming the values and behaviors in their children and serve as strong role models that greatly influence how a child will grow and develop. Parents choose the lifestyle: where children live, what they eat, where they go to school, and, at least in the younger years, who they play with.

For the young child, experts agree, the parent role is not that of a friend. They are the ones who set limits and establish expectations of behavior. Of course, parents can provide a good listening ear and empathize, but they need to draw the line at being a confidant. A confidant implies equality, which can undermine authority. Parents and children are not on the same level. With all their specific obligations and responsibilities, parents will find it harder to try to parent as a friend.

Grandparents come from a different place and speak with a different tone. We do speak with authority, wisdom, and perspective, yet from one generation removed from the parents. Since we are not the direct line of responsibility or authority, we have the luxury of being a friend and a confidant. We can be someone to turn to who helps make sense of the world. We can offer a safe haven in which to share more sensitive issues. Grandchildren listen to what a grandparent says with a special respect and tend to believe that what we say must be true (since we've grown so wise with age—ha!). After all, didn't we raise their mom or dad? We must know "better." That regard in itself brings a serious responsibility into the endeavor, a responsibility to the family as a whole.

It therefore becomes critical that we align with the parents and follow their lead. Working at odds with Mom or Dad or undermining their authority when caring for our grandchildren serves no one. We, too, must follow the rules and respect the boundaries and wishes of the parents even if we might disagree or think something should be done differently. We should always try to support their decisions, though we can support with a softer touch.

Of course, I identify with the children, too, and my balanced perspective gives me an advantage. I know where both sides are coming from—parent and child. I can see both sides as a result. That said, whenever there is a conflict, which is rare I'm happy to say, it's best to let them work it out together and without me. My role is not to interfere or discount anyone's feelings but to be a listening ear to my grandchildren so they know they are being heard. I actually see these moments of listening as a perfect opportunity to encourage our grandchildren to honor their parents, as we hope their parents honor us.

One time Lauren asked me if I was mad at her. I told her I never get mad at her, but sometimes I have to be firm. So now she reminds me to "be firm" with Daddy (my son) when he does something she knows I wouldn't like (for instance, leaving his shoes out to trip over or using a bad word). I get a kick out of hearing her say, "Grandma, you need to be firm with Daddy!" My son is a good sport and plays along with good humor. I'm sure he knows that this is yet another teaching moment that demonstrates listening to and respecting your parents, whatever your age. Sweetly, he'll move his shoes out of the doorway, showing me the respect he would like her to always show him.

In this triad, the parents' policies are the boundaries that children and grandparents alike work within. Not only is this best for the children but for the parents as well. They could do with some reinforcement. I am well aware and sympathetic to the challenges they face. There is no universal script on how to parent, so parents have to use their instincts and good judgment; most of the time that works, sometimes it doesn't. I know they might make a mistake or two when parenting, but so have I, and I can relate. What

I do know for certain is how deeply they want what is best for their children and family. They want to do what is right, so if they ever do get off track, I trust their intention and believe that they will learn how to do it better the next time. What they don't need is criticism from us (their parents) or an ongoing debate. Negative feedback is a brand killer for grandparenting.

And yes, of course I have found occasion to add my two cents, offering a suggestion or a different approach to my daughter or my son. (I'm still their parent, right?) But I try to do so only when asked or when a clear opportunity presents itself. They haven't disowned me yet, so I guess I haven't overstepped my bounds too many times.

THE VALUE OF GRANDPARENTS

Candidly, children don't *need* a grandparent, while they do need a parent (or two). But what a benefit we can be and a resource to them as well as to their parents. My grandchildren know that I don't have to be there but that I want to be. And I am happy that with the cooperation of their mom and dad, I get to be!

By being involved in our grandchildren's lives, we, too, are role models. Coming from another generation, grandparents can share another set of values and experiences, different from those of the parents. As a baby boomer, I can add the attributes of optimism, idealism, and a strong work ethic to the values of my grandkids' Generation X parents who crave independence and are more pragmatic, skeptical, and cautious. Layering these values is a tremendous benefit to the grandchildren, as it builds depth in character and perspective.

Children primarily learn their values by observing what you do and by listening to what you say. Sharing stories from your life experiences is a great way to transfer values.

"Grandma, were you ever mean to anyone?" Katie asked me one day.

"Well, I never meant to be mean to anyone, but I remember one time I did a mean thing to a friend in the third grade."

"What did you do?"

"We were waiting at the bus stop, and when she wasn't looking I put sow bugs in her purse," I recounted. "I thought it would be funny, but it wasn't funny to her. When she opened her purse, she was mad and very angry at me. I felt bad and was worried I would lose her as a friend. I didn't intend to do a mean thing, but it turned out I did."

"Did she forgive you?"

"Yes, she did. And she is still my friend because I told her I was sorry and I never did anything like that ever again. I learned that sometimes we hurt others when we don't intend to. Saying you're sorry and meaning it is always important."

My grandchildren love hearing this story of how my best childhood friend forgave me for putting sow bugs in her purse, or when my mother, as a young girl, had her mouth washed out with soap for lying to her mother, or how my adventuresome sister fried and ate grasshopper legs as a young girl (she said they tasted like popcorn!). A grandparent has a treasure trove of stories to share. And imbedded in these stories and experiences are our values and beliefs.

"Grandma, it's too windy today. I don't like the wind!" Jack exclaimed one time when I picked him up from school.

"I don't like it much either. I remember when I was a little girl the wind blew the door closed on my finger. It slammed shut and almost cut off the top. It hurt so bad, I was scared and crying."

"Grandma, what did you do?" he asked.

"I had to be brave. My mom and dad took me to the doctor, and he sewed the top of my finger back on."

"Then what did you do?"

"They took me to McDonald's for a hamburger, fries, and chocolate milkshake."

"Did it help?"

"Not much," I confessed. "But it was really nice of my parents to try to make me feel better."

These stories of our past are real; they are not imaginary tales from TV or movies. Why is this important? Because I've found that kids can better relate when it is about someone they know. They are learning as they listen to how you handled a situation, made decisions, and resolved mistakes. You can show them how you turned challenges into opportunities. They see that you survived, even if an event was painful. They can relate their own experiences to ones you had, whether it's hurting a friend, telling a lie, or falling in love for the first time. And from these connections, they gain a frame of reference about the world and feel less alone. Once you get started with stories, be prepared. Typically they want to hear favorite stories over and over and over. What a fabulous way to learn about life!

"Grandma, I have a crush on a boy," Lauren shared with me one time.

"Well, I was about your age when I got my first crush too."

"Oh, who was it? Who was it?" she begged me to tell her.

"His name was Roy Rogers, and he was King of the Cowboys!"

"Was Roy Rogers nice? Daddy said it's okay if I have a crush as long as the boy is nice."

"Oh yes, Roy Rogers was very, very nice, or so I'm told. You see, he was a movie star so I never met him."

"So he didn't know you liked him?"

"No, he never did."

"It's okay, Grandma, don't worry. I can keep your secret."

I think grandchildren know that for the most part grandparents are in their lives by choice. On some level, children understand that grandparents don't have to show up. If we do, hopefully it's because we want to. Typically, we are neither financially or legally responsible for the grandchildren's care and upbringing. So when we do spend time with them and make them a priority in our lives, they are bound to feel important. With all the choices available, and different ways grown-ups can spend their time, choosing to be with a grandchild must translate to them to mean, whether consciously or subconsciously, that they are special. And indeed, they are. And so is the grandparent for making them feel so.

Dr. Roma Hanks, professor of sociology, writes in her article, "Connecting the Generations: The New Role of Grandparents" for the Harbinger Foundation that:

"It is my belief that grandparenting is the most important family role of the new century. I say that because grandparents are just now discovering all the possibilities of relating to their grandchildren. Whether they are providing full-time care or working on a deeply supportive relationship, grandparents will have influence over a longer period of their grandchildren's lives than ever before. They will be healthier, more active, more involved, and more purposeful in relating to their grandchildren than were the grandparents that you and I knew. Their influence will spread beyond their own families."

As grandparents, we may not be able to save the world, but collectively we might just make our mark on its future.

ENTRY FROM MY JOURNAL, TUESDAY, JANUARY 15, 2013

Lauren woke up sick today and stayed home from school with me. She told her mom later that night, "Good thing I had my grandma today. She healed me."

CHAPTER TWENTY:

RAISE YOUR HAND!

F riends ask me how I got so involved with my grand-children. I tell them I raised my hand.

I knew I wanted more time with my grandchildren than seeing them on the occasional family visit or special holiday. It was clear to me that to have my own relationship with them would mean spending one-on-one time together, without Mom or Dad. Even when I am not needed to help with childcare, I ask for time with them. Whether it's for Camp Grandma (my house) or going to a play or another outing, whether it's with only one or all four grandchildren, being in their company is important to me. So I speak up and request time together. I don't wait for their parents to ask me.

It's not easy for today's parents to ask for help from their parents, other than an occasional babysitting job.

Sensitive about imposing, they understand we are living our "golden years" and hesitate to obligate us or tie us down. (We do treasure our independence and protect it at any cost—just ask a senior to give up her driver's license!) While parents theoretically may prefer the trusted grandparent for childcare, in practical terms they are often more comfortable hiring outside services. They need to be assured of the commitment, and it may seem easier to depend on someone who is paid and needs the job rather than count on volunteer help. In my own family, it took my daughter-in-law a couple of years before she finally realized I was serious about my commitment to help with regular childcare after she went back to work. Careful not to "impose" on me, or anyone for that matter, she tended to take on every responsibility herself. I'm much the same way, so I understood.

She'd say, "If you could help that would be great, but if you're busy, that's okay, I'll manage."

My response was, "I'll be there." And I was—and still am. Eventually she learned I wanted to be there and that I wanted to help. Fortunately, I live close by so that wasn't an issue. And hopefully by now she understands that this is by choice and a benefit for me too.

JUST OFFER

I know grandparents who are actually afraid to open the discussion with their children. They don't want to interfere or imply that the parents can't do it all themselves. Aware of how busy and active young families are today, they don't want to get in the way. So there is a good chance that in your world nobody is having the conversation relative to grand-parent and grandchildren spending time together. But it's not too late to change this—to broach the conversation and to see what might be needed.

If spending more time with your grandchildren is important to you, then start the conversation. I think it is the responsibility of the grandparent to help the parents understand this is a choice on your part—an intention, a desire, and a priority to play a loving role in the lives of your grandchildren. Raise your hand and then jump in. You can participate in their lives in some way that works. You might invent something unique to your circumstances. It hardly matters what the activities you choose might be. Your consistent presence and attention to and engagement with the kids is all that counts, and it makes a difference in enriching your life as well as theirs.

Maybe you begin by offering to help fill a need. When both parents work outside the home, they often need an afternoon/evening for themselves or a marriage retreat. Grandparents can (and do) play a major role with childcare and are often more flexible than hired help. Since most of us still drive, we can be of great value offering transportation to and from school and to meet special appointments.

Even if there is not a need, like help with childcare, time together with your grandchildren can be regularly arranged. Plan playdates with your own grandchildren. Invite them for a sleepover or out to lunch, or ask them to accompany you on any number of activities you would both enjoy. Whatever the circumstance, extended family is needed now more than ever, and your involvement would be a welcome gift and a win-win for all. Stepping up is the best way to begin building your own relationship with your grandchildren. Meanwhile, with their children in your trusted care, parents get some much-needed time to focus on other demands. And couldn't they use a break?

PARENTS NEED OUR HELP

I see the pressure and stress of our society bearing down on today's parents in the faces of my daughter and son. The pace they keep is incredible. Not only is their generation responsible for raising the children but also for looking after their parents, a generation living longer than ever before.

Born between 1965 and 1984, my offspring and their friends are part of Generation X. Common characteristics include marrying later in life, consequently being older when they have their first child, and coming from smaller, more fractured families. They are also referred to as the "sandwich generation," feeling pressure from the top (parents) and pressure from below (children).

Many, if not most, are two-income families, with both parents in demanding jobs or professions. More is expected of them at work with technology playing a big part in the demand for performance 24/7. Moms used to go to work because they wanted an outside job or to help their families get ahead. Now it appears two jobs are needed to just stay afloat. Parents today appear to run around with their "hair on fire" much of the time, overwhelmed and overloaded with careers, childcare, and social pressures, not to mention the expectation of always looking "trim and fit" while doing it all!

Even managing their children's schedules can be a full-time job, balancing the full load of activities, interests, therapies, and sports. Kids don't "go out and play" in their neighborhoods anymore. Now the parents have to arrange playdates, on top of soccer games, dance classes, music lessons, and more. I'm exhausted even thinking about it. Is it any wonder that finding a livable work-life balance seems like an impossible dream? I have a special appreciation of how difficult it must be for a single parent. One can only hope they have support from family or friends willing to pitch in and contribute. Without help, I have no idea how they do it all.

When I hear other grandparents choosing not to be involved and saying, "I raised mine," I truly understand and respect their decision. But I contend that times have changed. Life today is different. Our kids aren't raising their children in the same world we did. So much more is expected. More assistance is required. More support is appreciated. Who better to lend a hand than a grandparent?

A dear friend once told me, "Do the work that only you can do. Figure out what is special about you and consider what you have to contribute." For me, I know my value as a grandparent. Fortunately, I have the opportunity, ability, and energy to add support. Not to mention, I have the stories, the history, the commitment, and unwavering love to share.

I remember someone saying, "I allow for my children's success." I always liked that sentiment. I want to pave the way for my family's happiness. I believe that everything we teach them, all the lessons they learn, are in an effort to help them find the health, fulfillment, and joy they seek. As models and mentors we can show how this is possible.

This isn't about "doing" for them. They have to travel their own journey of life, taking personal responsibility, making their own decisions, and suffering through their own mistakes. But I can help provide necessary tools and run interference when appropriate.

And it's not about "enabling" them. I'm not suggesting shifting accountability or making allowances that shield consequences. It's more like giving them permission, the green light to be, to dream, and to accomplish. My daughter once remarked that for her, I'm like the song by Bette Midler, "Wind beneath My Wings." I was flattered by the reference, and I'm happy to help propel and inspire my family to achieve the success they desire.

ALL YOU NEED IS LOVE

I understand some families live across the country from each other or are unable to make regular visits for other reasons. As many as 50 percent of grandparents live more than two hundred miles away from their grandchildren; many are still working and view lack of time as a constraint. Health issues can also be a determining factor on how active you can be. Though challenging, these circumstances don't have to keep a grandparent from being involved in the most important way, through the connection of love.

It's important to note that Camp Grandma does not have to be an actual physical place. It's at its core a state of mind, an intention to connect lovingly. It's an opportunity for grandchildren to come together in hearts and minds with their grandparents to learn and share experience. It exists in the heart, the place of many far-reaching inner connectors.

If you feel there are limiting factors to your ability to have a good effect on your grandchildren and a good experience for yourself, I offer a few suggestions. I have friends who reach out through social media, or they Skype, FaceTime, or text with their grandchildren to stay connected. But they don't just rely on the new tools of technology. They use the old tools, too, the ones we grew up with, like the phone or letter writing. Maybe you could become pen pals or share books to read, creating your own book club. You might consider learning a new language together and exchange simple dialogue in letters or on the phone. You could write stories to document family heritage and history or start a collection of favorite family recipes.

On your grandchild's birthday, along with the birthday card, send a picture of yourself at that age. Tell something about you that you recall during that time of your life. Ask for a story or a drawing in return in which your grandchild might tell you about the year just past or what they look forward to in the coming year. You will learn something about each other with each exchange, and if done regularly, these will become building blocks of your growing relationship.

There are lots of innovative ideas on the Internet for long-distance grandparents seeking meaningful ways to connect with their grandchildren, from trading postcards via snail mail to creating your own fantasy sports league. Pick an interest you can share together and invest the time to keep the communication going and your grandchildren emotionally close.

Anyone can build their own Camp Grandma (or Camp Grandpa). Just adapt the activities scattered throughout this book to your own needs and particular style. It may feel like we are in our "last act," but we can start our "new act" through our involvement with our grandchildren. We all want to feel needed, that we have a purpose. Is there any greater legacy than the one before you? Just look; it's already there. You created new life in your offspring, and from them has come more. You raised them as best you could, and now they are raising their legacy to the world. You are now in a position to help, influence, and support. That can be very gratifying and rewarding.

IT'S YOUR TURN

At this stage of life, it's only natural to want to make an imprint, to have an effect and be regarded for your good works. Ultimately, we'd all like to be remembered in a positive and loving way. But how that happens is up to you. There is no one right way to do it. It's your way. In this book, I'm suggesting a flexible framework within which to build your own Camp Grandma atop a foundation I've tested and found tried and true. But again, the content is up to you, based on your own platform and experiences of life.

So I invite you to go on a Camp Grandma adventure, your adventure and one within your reach, adjusted to fit your circumstances. There are children everywhere who need love and attention, and some is better than none, both for the giver and the receiver. There is some way you can begin now on a journey that, at the very least, will be life enhancing. It could turn out to be life changing, if you decide to go all the way as I did and function as a mentor.

Mark Twain is credited with the quote, "The two most important days of your life are the day you were born and the day you find out why." Grandparents can definitely assist their grandchildren in understanding the why. We might even better understand our whys as well in the process.

CHAPTER TWENTY-ONE:

WHAT'S NEXT?

I know I am lucky to live close to my family. I know I'm fortunate to be able to share in their lives and watch my grandchildren grow up. Before my eyes, they are maturing and changing so fast they keep me running to catch up. It wasn't so long ago when my grandchildren used to say, "Wait for me, Grandma," Jake scurrying to collect his books, Lauren rushing to grab her toy baby stroller to take on walks, Katie always a couple steps behind, Jack at the door. Now I'm the one quietly asking them to wait for me as I watch the years quickly pass.

Camp Grandma is changing too. It has to. It has evolved right along with the four of them. I started modifying the activities to reflect their ages and interests pretty early on. We formally started Camp Grandma when the kids were ten, eight, seven, and five. Five years in, with a teenager in the ranks, I can introduce more mature subjects, along with expanding on our current themes and activities. My focus will continue to be on personal development.

I mentioned that I was lucky. So are my grandchildren. I want them to appreciate their good health and bright minds. Life for each of them is so abundant with loving and caring parents, an extended family to offer support and security in belonging, not to mention the good fortune to be born with the freedoms and opportunities afforded us here in the United States of America. I'd like to help them appreciate who they are today as a result of their many blessings. And looking forward, I am curious to know who they might want to become and what a happy life would look like.

We can do this by introducing the concepts of character and values. By introducing values through fun exercises, we can start talking about who they are today and the person they want to be when they grow up, *their future selves.* This pairs up nicely with their résumés, where we work on *the life they want.* Wouldn't it be nice if they could live their life by intention rather than reaction or just "going with the flow"?

At a recent Camp Grandma, when we were all sitting on the back patio, I began to ask questions:

"How would you describe yourself?"

"Describe Grandma."

"What does it take to be happy as a grown-up?"

I then introduced a simple activity where I listed for them ten to twenty of the most common values, like honesty, loyalty, and patience, to name a few. I asked them to circle five that they thought were most important in guiding their actions and behavior. There were no right or wrong answers, just whatever they chose that would lead to some intriguing conversation. From there we built on the discussion. My goal was to get them thinking about values and the qualities of the people they'd like to be.

I chuckled at the responses they came up with. Katie, Jake, and Jack all said they were smart, funny, and creative. But it was Lauren who decided to improvise when describing herself. She said, "I think I am pretty and loyal and friendly and I am amazing!" I hope she never loses that perspective. When I asked her about Grandma, she remarked, "Grandmas are persons with excellent cleaning skills." (I'm so glad she noticed!)

I love that I can ask the kids questions now whenever we are together and it doesn't have to be within the formal structure of Camp Grandma. They are used to me doing or asking the unexpected, so they are not startled when I make the query, "How do you think your friends would describe you today?" We know how important it is to ask questions. It's fun for me to think of new ones to keep challenging their brains in different ways.

In time I'd like to introduce other, more practical, themes. One that is important to learn is how to manage money (budgeting and the value of saving and sharing). As they acquire income through allowances, gifts, or even babysitting, they will have to make choices on how to use it. Kids don't typically learn this in school, and an early education can provide important skills for the rest of their lives. Other ideas I have for Camp Grandma include discussions on creating a positive self-image, the value of time management, and learning to be your own advocate.

CHANGING THE WORLD

So what do I think will come of all of this? For my grandchildren, hopefully a richer life. Maybe an idea or two will sink in or trigger a spark of interest they might like to pursue. A situation might arise where they can draw from an experience or skill set they learned at Camp Grandma. At the very least, I hope they will be better prepared for life and will have learned the value of family.

Ultimately, I hope to encourage in my grandchildren the desire to contribute to the world in some way, large or small, rather than "just take up space." I'd like them to feel they have a purpose for being here. I know, that sounds overwhelming—it's a daunting task at any age to feel you have to discover your one big purpose for living. So I tell them there can be more than one purpose, depending on where you are in life. Discovering your purpose is a lifetime journey, a hopeful, continuous endeavor that leads to a more meaningful life.

I've always liked the quote by Ralph Waldo Emerson: "To leave the world a bit better, whether by a healthy child, a garden patch, or a redeemed social condition; to know that even one life has breathed easier because you have lived—that is to have succeeded."

Of course, the easiest way to do this is to leave everything better than you found it. I had an experience in high school that perfectly demonstrates this concept. I had a part-time job at a local movie theater after school. I started working behind the candy counter but quickly moved up to selling tickets. My friend thought it would be fun to work there too, so I recommended her to the manager. She got the job and replaced me selling candy and popcorn.

Now, I knew I did an adequate job in that position. I was competent, honest, and friendly with the customers and kept my work area clean and tidy. But when my friend took over the job, I noticed she did all of that and more. When her shift was done, she always had fresh popcorn made and filled to the top of the popcorn maker and had all the candy stocked to the fullest, ready for the next employee when their shift would start. Why did this impress me as important? Because she did the *most* she could do. She exceeded expectations without being told to. She left the place better than she found it. I have never forgotten that experience and, to this day, try to follow her example. It may seem rather trivial, but it had a profound impact on me. It told me no job is trivial if a person of character is doing it.

Life is about making a difference no matter how small it may seem. The Internet is full of ideas on how to make a difference: starting a charity, volunteering, working in animal shelters, donating old toys and clothing, and so forth. Children can begin now, by walking their dog, finding ways to help Mom or Dad, or simply picking up a piece of trash. The interesting thing is that kids often want to help, to earn money, to participate—they start out eager to be a part of things.

I'm suggesting that we consider every day to be an opportunity to make our mark, by contributing and adding value. Every day we can take pause and ask what difference we made that day. You may not bring peace to the world or cure cancer, but a simple act of kindness can make a difference. Introducing this concept to children early in life might just change the world.

I'm excited to see where life will take my grandchildren, what they choose to do and who they will become. I'm certainly in no hurry for them to grow up, though they'll do that anyway. I will always try to stay close but will continue to view them differently than when I raised my own children. Clearly, my lens has shifted. I have no expectations for my grandchildren. They will be who they will be. I don't expect them to turn out a certain way, attend certain colleges, or have a specific occupation.

I do have hope for them, which is different than expectation. Hope is an optimistic attitude that feels bright and light to me. It's more of a compelling desire than a static assumption. With hope, I can wish them every blessing without the limits of predetermined expectations.

All I can be sure of for my grandchildren is that they will have me and the gifts of my time and experience as long as I am able and they want me. I will be there as a coach, a mentor, a sounding board, and for a warm hug. And I'll be the first to remind them if I feel they are behaving in ways that don't reflect the terrific people I know them to be.

I recently had dinner with Jack and his family, celebrating my daughter's birthday. We were talking about kids and drugs. He laughed out loud and said, "I'll never do drugs 'cause I know Grandma would come after me for sure!" He's got that right; Jack knows me well.

CHAPTER TWENTY-TWO:

WHAT'S LOVE GOT TO DO WITH IT?

Bob and Cheryl dedicate their Saturdays to sitting on bleachers to watch their grandchildren play varied team sports.

Gail and Glenn planned a whole summer on the road, traveling with their grandson to show him the United States.

Jo Bonita has a file folder where she keeps her scrapbook of memories to review with her grandchildren periodically.

Dodie collects team T-shirts throughout the young lives of her eight grandchildren. From the fabric of these shirts she makes each a quilt to present to them on their eighteenth birthday.

Barbara sends beautifully illustrated books to her grandchildren, who live three thousand miles away, with a personal inscription in each as a connection and remembrance.

Jim and Dana are in perpetual motion traveling from one coast to the other, with stops in between, so they don't miss a single milestone in their grandchildren's lives.

Greg, a retired NFL offensive guard, waits by a locked gate to pick up his granddaughter from preschool.

Patti makes shopping for school clothes an annual event.

Kathy and Bob run a fishing academy for their two grandsons for one week every summer in the Boundary Waters of northern Minnesota.

Sherry returns from Africa so inspired that she sponsors four African children and connects them with her four grandchildren here in the States of similar age. She's creating an opportunity for her grandchildren to give back, learn compassion, and develop friendships on the other side of the world.

I could go on and on with examples of how grandparents connect with their grandchildren. Grandparents do the most amazing and selfless things all the time. These stories don't make the news, but maybe they should. Because on a daily basis, with each lullaby, each story told, each moment together or connection from afar, grandparents are able to transfer wisdom, accumulated knowledge, family history, culture, multigenerational values, and unconditional love.

THE ROLE OF GRANDPARENTS

What is wrong with our society that it doesn't place more value on the grandparent role? Is it oblivious to what we have to offer? It's concerning that culturally there's too much emphasis on youth. People past a certain age are treated as irrelevant, almost invisible. In other countries, the grandparent is more highly esteemed. In Vietnam, for instance, the grandparent is the most respected role in the family. Many Asian cultures follow codes of behavior that include reverence for ancestors and respect for elders. In India, the ancient Vedic scripture outlines a one-hundred-year plan for mankind, which highlights the value of those over age fifty. People in this age group are highly respected for their knowledge and experience. Rather than being "put out to pasture," they are responsible for helping not only their families but also society as a whole. In Greek culture, old age is celebrated, and I've been told it is actually a compliment to be called an "old man." So maybe the conversation needs to be about how our society treats the elderly (ouch, not my favorite description of myself), but that's another story.

We need to turn some attention to grandparenting—what it is and what it can be. The grandparent will remain an untapped resource as long as we continue to overlook and underutilize this most effective advocate for a loving society. In today's busy, harried, and technology-driven world, grandparents can and do play a major role by providing wisdom, strength, comfort, and security as part of an extended family.

A dear friend of mine read my manuscript and remarked, "I hope this doesn't make other grandparents feel bad that they can't do for their grandchildren what you do with yours at Camp Grandma." Well, that would make me so very sad if that were the case because what I intend to demonstrate is how limitless the role of a grandparent can be. My stories reflect only me. With my grandchildren, I share what I've learned, drawing from my own experiences to add value to their lives. My background has been as a businesswoman, so I felt qualified—and thought it would be interesting and fun—to introduce several of the more timeless business principals to them. I'm not suggesting others should do exactly the same thing I've done. Yet from this demonstration of how I approach the role of a grandparent others can (and do) share their own talents in their own way. I hope the activities I've included provide a springboard for you in your own efforts.

There are grandparents from different walks of life who bring their unique selves to their relationships with their grandchildren. Whatever the profession (nurse, lawyer, teacher, fireman) or whatever the background (PTA chairman, YMCA volunteer, Sunday school teacher), I hope my example might encourage them to engage their grandchildren in ways reflective of them, in addition to the more traditional grandparent activities, like crafts, playing, or babysitting. My way is just that, my way, and if I happen to spark an idea or inspiration for someone else, then I've accomplished my goal.

By directing a spotlight on the role of the grandparent, I mean to applaud all the fabulous ways grandparents are making a contribution to this world. Though these efforts often go unnoticed and unrecognized in our society, their own families are grateful, I'm sure. I know hardly a day goes by without me hearing a heartfelt thank-you from my family. Of course, my biggest thank-you comes from my opportunity to be with my grandchildren. As

I've already said, my joy comes from being a part of their lives and building a multigenerational bond that will last a lifetime. I know other grandparents feel the same way.

BUILDING A BOND

Anthropologist Margaret Mead reportedly said that connections between the generations are "essential for the mental health and stability of a nation."

The grandparent role is vital in our society today. We are a critical link that connects the past with the present, and we can influence the future as well. When we share our memories and stories with our grandchildren, they are able to capture bits of history that might otherwise be lost. Families can pass down culture and tradition. We are the foundation on which to build not only the family but also the framework of our society, by transmitting values and norms of social order.

Granted, not all grandparents have the wherewithal or desire to be close to their grandchildren. These grandparents probably aren't reading this book. But for the rest of us, the role of the grandparent is limited only by our imagination. We don't have to settle for tired, stereotypical traditions. We can create new ones. We don't have to exist on the periphery. We can be in the thick of it! With a greater appreciation of the possibilities, the grandparent role can have even greater impact than it does today.

True, we can babysit. This helps Mom and Dad. But let's not forget what we are doing for our grandchildren. We are helping to shape their minds and build skills in preparation for the real world. We are grounding them with a sense of place and identity. We are influencing, through our personal experience and perspective, their behavioral and social development inspiring them to be well-rounded individuals. Do we babysit? Sure, but clearly grandparents have the capacity to do so much more.

What do we ourselves gain by being in the good company of our grandchildren? Purpose and relevance. By engaging with youth, we stay younger longer. Our hearts grow stronger from building loving relationships. We stay more active. We have something else to think about other than our own aches, pains, and diminished capacity. I know I am forming deep bonds and relationships that will outlive me. Maybe one of my grandchildren will tell the story of Camp Grandma to their grandchildren. Maybe they will introduce me to them through mentioning my favorite flower (the rose), my favorite color (pink), or my favorite fragrance (lavender). Maybe one day they'll do their own Camp Grandma or Camp Grandpa for their own grandchildren.

The world is changing so fast now; it's hard to imagine what my grandchildren will be like in twenty years, let alone fifty. I do accept that as adults with their own families and friends, they won't be thinking about me every day. That is how it should be. Hopefully they will be independent and responsible, with self-sustaining skills and values that will shape the rest of their lives. But how do I measure the countless little ways I have influenced them? I know I have played a key role in their development. Grandma was there, "helping us all cheer up," as Jack would say. From the day they were born I was a part of their lives. And for the rest of my life, they will be a part of mine.

EPILOGUE

My grandchildren continue to open my eyes and teach me lessons worth repeating, one of which is to avoid the words *no, not, never, can't, won't*. When I must be instructional, I try not to tell them what *not* to do, but rather what *to* do. For example, "Please close the door," rather than, "Don't leave the door open!" works so much better.

Businesses and corporate environments that need creative people would do well to remember that too. In a way, it's the difference between being a babysitter ("No, don't do that") and being a mentor ("Go ahead, do it if you can, or try this"). If you really believe what you're doing is valuable, then why not go all the way with it? If you're spending your time caretaking, then raise the stakes and make it a mentoring experience. Mentoring helps people learn, and don't we have a lot to learn?

Candidly, I don't think humans are very good students. Oh sure, we can learn a lot, like how to read and write. But to be wise? It appears we all have to learn that for ourselves. Yet if I could impart some additional bits of wisdom that I have gleaned in my life and save my grandchildren from the pain of learning it firsthand, I offer the following:

- Learn the difference between having the right to say something and saying something that is right.
- Sit up front! Don't cower in the back of the room as if ready for a quick getaway. The view is better up front, and you won't miss anything. Furthermore, the teacher can't ignore you when you want to ask another question.
- Do the hard stuff first. Do yourself a favor and get your work done early so you have plenty of free time for play.
- Look your best. If you dress like a slob, you are apt to behave like one.
- If you aren't happy, fake it. People around you don't want to be punished if you happen to wake up on the wrong side of the bed.
- Take care of your teeth. They were not made for opening bottle caps or splitting apart Lego pieces. Tip: learn to floss early in life.
- Take your time growing up. Trust me on this— one day you'll be willing to give all you have to be the young age you once were.
- Pay attention to Mom and Dad. They really do want what is best for you and don't speak to hear themselves talk.

- Respect our planet. It's the best home you will ever have.
- Make something of your life—only you can do it.
- If you want financial wealth, then don't spend more than you make.
- Best not to feel sorry for yourself—it's a waste of energy. I guarantee you, someone somewhere is having a worse day.
- Respect others. Remember, they are just you in a different body.
- Holding a grudge hurts you more than anyone else.
- Be the first to say you are sorry, and mean it.
- Don't be in such a big hurry to get what you want. My father used to remind me, "Anticipation is greater than realization." More times than not, he was right.
- Follow your heart, but use your head to show you the way.
- Count your blessings every day. Start with Mom and Dad, or the new puppy or video game. Just start—and never stop.

INDEX

ACKNOWLEDGMENTS

I f anyone had ever said I would one day author a book, I would have laughed out loud and shaken my head in disbelief. But after being prompted by five good friends to tell my grandmother story, that is exactly what happened. Of course, I didn't do it alone. This wouldn't have happened without the help and encouragement of so many wonderful people. To all of you, a heartfelt thank-you.

To Gloria Loring, Cindy Swain, Jo Bonita Rains, Carol Schillne, and Julie Bernstein, you were the five that believed I had something to say, as well as being readers of my early formats, rooting me on along the way.

To Sherry Bower, Laree Kiely, Robert Leech, Nancy Lavelle, Gloria Wolen, Michele Day, Emily Devor, and Sharon Goldinger, all readers, advisors, and supportive friends that encouraged me to continue.

To Ondra Gilbertson, for her friendship and support at countless Camp Grandmas.

To Kelly Murphy, always my partner—whether advising, collaborating, or conspiring.

To Candace Hogan, my blood sister, lifelong friend, and editor, who made it happen with her wisdom and expertise, painstakingly guiding me along the way to create the book you're reading today.

To my publisher, Brooke Warner, many thanks to you and your excellent team at She Writes Press.

To my daughter, Laurie; her husband, Pat; my son, David; and his wife, Susan, for sharing their precious children with me and trusting in my ability to tell our Camp Grandma story.

To my husband, Art, who never once questioned I could pull this off, while lovingly helping me through every step in the process.

ABOUT THE AUTHOR

As a young wife and stay-at-home mother, Marianne Waggoner Day was a "typical" June Cleaver housewife of the '60s and '70s—until her divorce necessitated getting a job. She started her career in sales and was promoted to various management positions. Ultimately, she became president of retail services for CBRE, where she led the largest commercial retail real estate practice in the world. Under her management, it outperformed the competition nearly two to one.

Marianne was the first woman to earn a Lifetime Achievement Award at the one-hundred-year-old company. She was a frequent speaker and facilitated learning and training sessions. Ten years ago, she elected to step down from her corporate role while continuing to consult with former clients and coach high-performing business professionals.

Now in retirement, she has come full circle—from having her picture in the *Wall Street Journal* to spending much of her day caring for her grandchildren.

Not exciting? You may be surprised. She started Camp Grandma for her four grandchildren and created lessons and activities from what she knows best. What evolved was a child's version of a corporate retreat, where she uses fun and engaging ways to teach valuable life skills, such as setting goals, being a team player, and speaking in front of a group.

Along the way, she observed the often diminished and undervalued role of the grandparent in our society today. Grandparents are so much more than babysitters. Marianne wants to be a voice that elevates their "brand," inspiring ways to unlock even greater potential in the role.

Author photo © Wayne Wright

SELECTED TITLES FROM SHE WRITES PRESS

She Writes Press is an independent publishing company founded to serve women writers everywhere. Visit us at www.shewritespress.com.

The Clarity Effect: How Being More Present Can Transform Your Work and Life by Sarah Harvey Yao. $16.95, 978-1-63152-958-0. A practical, strategy-filled guide for stressed professionals looking for clarity, strength, and joy in their work and home lives.

I Know It In My Heart: Walking through Grief with a Child by Mary E. Plouffe. $16.95, 978-1631522000. Every child will experience loss; every adult wants to know how to help. Here, psychologist Mary E. Plouffe uses her own family's tragic loss to tell the story of childhood grief—its expression and its evolution—from ages three to fifteen.

Loving Lindsey: Raising a Daughter with Special Needs by Linda Atwell. $16.95, 978-1631522802. A mother's memoir about the complicated relationship between herself and her strong-willed daughter, Lindsey—a high-functioning young adult with intellectual disabilities.

Godmother: An Unexpected Journey, Perfect Timing, and Small Miracles by Odile Atthalin. $16.95, 978-1-63152-172-0. After thirty years of traveling the world, Odile Atthalin—a French intellectual from a well-to-do family in Paris—ends up in Berkeley, CA, where synchronicities abound and ultimately give her everything she has been looking for, including the gift of becoming a godmother.

Mothering Through the Darkness: Women Open Up About the Postpartum Experience edited by Stephanie Sprenger and Jessica Smock. $16.95, 978-1-63152-804-0. A collection of thirty powerful essays aimed at spreading awareness and dispelling myths about postpartum depression and perinatal mood disorders.

Renewable: One Woman's Search for Simplicity, Faithfulness, and Hope by Eileen Flanagan. $16.95, 978-1-63152-968-9. At age forty-nine, Eileen Flanagan had an aching feeling that she wasn't living up to her youthful ideals or potential, so she started trying to change the world—and in doing so, she found the courage to change her life.